VOLUME THREE

CLASSIC GUNFIGHTS

WRITTEN AND ILLUSTRATED BY
BOB BOZE BELL

MAPS & GRAPHICS BY GUS WALKER

ORIGINAL PHOTOGRAPHS
FROM THE COLLECTION OF ROBERT G. McCUBBIN

First Edition • May 2007
Published by Tri Star - Boze Publications, Inc. • 3110 North 35th Avenue, Suite 4 • Phoenix, Arizona 85017
602-269-2900 • 800-350-6345 • Facsimile 602-269-1469
ISBN 978-1-887576-12-3 (Soft Cover) • ISBN 978-1-887576-13-0 (Hardbound)

APACHE KID

OTHERS FOUGHT TO THE LAST MAN...
(OR DID THEY?)

DAVY CROCKETT AND CUSTER

SOME WERE NOT EVEN FROM AMERICA...

BEN THOMPSON FROM ENGLAND

BUTCH CASSIDY, THE SUNDANCE KID AND ETTA PLACE

WILD BILL HICKOK

JEFF MILTON

TABLE OF CONTENTS

92

AST OR SLOW, DRUNK OR SOBER, UGLY OR
VAIN, THE GUNFIGHTERS ARE GONE NOW...
BUT THE TALES OF THEIR COURAGE REMAIN.

JOHN WESLEY HARDIN

HELL'S IN SESSION!

⸻ ☆ ⸻

26 SHOOT-OUTS VS 757 LEGENDS

⸻ ☆ ⸻

This, my third volume of *Classic Gunfights*, is the most ambitious yet. I made a conscious decision to expand the coverage and include bigger shoot-outs such as the Battle of the Little Bighorn and the Alamo. True, I am stretching the definition of a "gunfight," but I believe the format keeps it all in line: great photos, readable maps, authentic illustrations and a no-nonsense narrative serve my goal: to make sense of complicated events, all of them shrouded in myth and legend. I think it's safe to say the 26 gunfights in this book have spawned at least 757 legends (with the Battle of the Little Bighorn possibly achieving that number all by its lonesome).

Although I have thanked all of the researchers and authors who assisted me with these gunfights in the back of this book, several must be thanked for contributions far beyond the call of duty.

Paul Andrew Hutton provided much needed expertise and recommended other experts for two of his passions: The Alamo and the Little Bighorn fight. One of them was Michael Donahue, who has uncovered compelling evidence of Custer's final movements beyond Custer Hill. He and history buff Jim Hatzell gave me a personal tour of the Little Bighorn Battlefield which really expanded my understanding of this complicated battle (p. 118).

Dan Buck and Anne Meadows allowed me to utilize their primary research on Butch and Sundance. Their incredible collection of South American photographs and artifacts is truly amazing. In turn, Gus Walker created a remarkable map of the outlaws' final run (p. 38).

One of Len Gratteri's areas of interest is Medicine Lodge, Kansas, and his rare photos of the Medicine Lodge Bank and the local livery stables, businesses and area cowboys really help to flesh out that gunfight. Likewise, local residents of Medicine Lodge, Dillman Ash and Beverly McCollom, corrected many misconceptions about the famous bank robbery and chase. Dillman even took me out to the canyon where the robbers were captured (p. 66).

No one I have met knows the history of Caldwell, Kansas, better than Rod Cook. His contributions to the convoluted events during the Talbot Gang shoot-out really give that gunfight some clarity (p. 92).

Longtime *True West* contributor and master artist Gary Zaboly has created some of the best overviews of the Alamo. He graciously allows me to republish them here to great effect (p. 28).

True West Features Editor Mark Boardman helped out with more than one gunfight, directing me to the most accurate accounts and researchers, such as Tom Bicknell who has studied the deadly Thompson brothers and knows their escapades better than anyone else (p. 98). He also recommended Jim Gray, who infused my coverage of the Ellsworth fight, both with historical detail and a great photo comparison of old Ellsworth and the modern version of the town (p. 72).

Leon Metz, always gracious, answered many questions about John Wesley Hardin's final days (p. 80).

John Boessenecker and Bill Secrest, Sr. are my go-to guys whenever the subject is California outlaws. And John's knowledge of the details surrounding the Kingston robbery and shoot-out is nothing short of exemplary (p. 62).

When it comes to Billy the Kid and the Lincoln County War, no one knows more about this convoluted and contradictory saga than Fred Nolan. And he always answers my questions with style and wit (p. 32, 60).

Paul Cool shared his massive research and his rare images on the Salt War, and all of this before the publication of his forthcoming book (p. 112).

I recently ran across an intriguing concept that applies to all of the Wild West characters featured in the *Classic Gunfights* series. Here it is:

"The more different kinds of stories and even contradictory stories that can be told about someone, the more famous he will be." —Leo Braudy

—BOB BOZE BELL
CAVE CREEK, AZ

BLACK BART'S BAD DAY

---☆---

BLACK BART VS REASON MCCONNELL & JIMMY ROLLERI

---☆---

THINGS GET FUNKY ON FUNK HILL

---☆---

*"I've labored long and hard for bread
For honor and for riches
But on my corns too long you've tread
You fine haired sons of bitches."*

—BLACK BART, THE P o 8

It's a Saturday as the Sonora-Milton stage rattles along, empty, save for the driver. Reason E. McConnell has been on the road for three hours since he stopped at the Patterson Mine, near Tuttletown, California, picking up $4,200 worth of amalgamated gold. The Wells Fargo box also contains $500 in gold coin and $64 in raw gold.

McConnell finally reins up in front of the Reynolds Ferry Hotel, nestled along the banks of the Stanislaus River. Jimmy Rolleri, the hotel manager's 19-year-old son, exits the hotel and exchanges the outgoing mail for the incoming. Glancing at the empty coach, Rolleri asks if he can catch a ride up the hill on the opposite side of the river. A traveler who had stopped at the hotel the previous night reported seeing "two big bucks up there on the flat above Yaqui Gulch," he says.

McConnell tells the boy to grab his gun, and Rolleri returns with a "well-worn but serviceable .44 Henry rifle." With the help of Henry Requa, the two successfully ferry the stage across the river. Requa returns the ferry to the hotel side of the river, and Rolleri jumps up on the box with McConnell, who slaps the reins of his team, encouraging them up the steep approach to Funk Hill.

Halfway up the long grade, Rolleri asks McConnell to slow down. He jumps off with his rifle, thanks McConnell for the lift and heads out into the underbrush to hunt for the big bucks.

The six-horse team continues on, struggling up the steep grade for another 30 minutes. As the stage rounds the head of Yaqui Gulch, with the ridge line in sight, the lead horses snort and rear in fright when a lone, hooded figure, shotgun in hand, leaps into the roadway.

Wearing a dirt-smudged duster and a flour sack with eye holes cut into them, the highwayman demands the Wells Fargo box be thrown down. McConnell informs the robber it's bolted down. The outlaw tells the driver to unhitch his team, but McConnell protests, fearing the stage will roll down the hill due to its bad brakes. The robber's solution is for McConnell to wedge rocks behind the wheels, but the driver brashly pushes his luck by stating, "Why don't you do it?"

Incredibly, the hooded robber keeps his shotgun trained on the driver, picks up several stones and blocks the back wheels. McConnell then unhitches the team and leads it uphill. "If you don't want to get shot," the robber warns him, "don't come back or even look back in this direction for at least one hour."

While leading the team, McConnell hears the robber banging away at the strongbox. Sneaking glances toward the coach, he can't see the brigand, who has probably crawled into the stagecoach.

Two hundred yards from the stage, McConnell stops to catch his breath when downhill movement catches his eye. It's Jimmy Rolleri, the Henry rifle in the crook of his arm, moving across an open swale of land about 300 yards below. Tying his team to an oak tree, McConnell runs downhill as quietly as he can, frantically waving his hat until he gets Rolleri's attention. Coming up the hill, Rolleri first thinks McConnell has discovered the deer. But the driver fills him in on the situation, and the two warily approach the stage with the intent of capturing the outlaw, or killing him. When they get within 100 yards, the bandit suddenly emerges from the stage and spots them. The outlaw throws a sack over his shoulder and starts to run.

McConnell borrows Rolleri's rifle and fires twice, missing the robber both times.

"Here, let me shoot," young Rolleri says. "I'll get him and I won't kill him, either." With Rolleri's shot, the outlaw stumbles, but he vanishes into the underbrush with his booty.

When the county sheriff and a Wells Fargo detective arrive, they discover what the brigand left behind in his hasty retreat: a derby hat, three pairs of cuffs, an opera glass case and a silk crepe handkerchief with the laundry mark "F.X.O.7." on it.

After eight years and 28 successful stage holdups, this last item will prove to be Black Bart's undoing.

When his photo is taken in Stockton, Black Bart quips: "Will that thing go off? I would like to go off myself."

A Dapper Disguise

Looking more like a banker than a common stage robber, Black Bart cuts a distinguished figure around San Francisco (his hideout), where he poses as a mining investor named Charles Bolton.

The Monday after the stage robbery, Detective Harry Morse begins matching laundry marks from a handkerchief left at the scene with those of the 91 laundry centers in San Francisco. By the afternoon, he has a match. When a nattily-dressed suspect is taken to Wells Fargo headquarters, the agents are shocked as he looks like "anything but a stage robber." By the end of the week, Black Bart confesses and leads officers to the buried gold. He also poses for the above photograph.

By all accounts, the bandit is witty, self-effacing and intelligent. He even writes a letter from prison to Reason McConnell, who he thanks for being such a lousy shot. He ends the warm letter with: "You sir, have my best wishes for an unmolested, prosperous and happy drive through life."

Black Bart's Odd Style

While most stage robbers ride horses for a faster getaway, Bart walks. And unlike most, he acts alone (not an easy task considering the multiple factors to control: the horses, the road, the driver and the passengers). At two of the robbery sites, he leaves zany poetry, signing it: "Black Bart, the Po8."

Wells Fargo officials admit that the bandit poet hit the company 28 times. Although the total amount of money stolen is unknown, here's a listing of his known robberies and amounts taken.

The Great Stage Robberies

1. July 26, 1875, Calaveras County
Four miles from Copperopolis, California, Charles E. Boles robs the stagecoach enroute to Milton. **Taken:** $160 in gold notes and the contents of a U.S. Mail pouch.

2. December 28, 1875, Yuba County
North San Juan to Marysville, California, stage. **Taken:** Small undetermined amount of cash.

3. June 2, 1876, Siskiyou County
A nighttime robbery on the Roseburg, Oregon, to Yreka, California, route. **Taken:** $80 and an unknown amount from mail sacks.

4. August 3, 1877, Sonoma County
Between Fort Ross and Duncan Mills, on the Russian River. **Taken:** $300 in gold coins and a check for $305. **Poem:** First poem discovered.

5. July 25, 1878, Butte County
The Quincy to Oroville, California, stage. **Taken:** $379 in coins, a $200 diamond ring, $25 silver watch and cash from mail sacks. **Poem:** Second poem found (printed on opposite page).

6. July 30, 1878, Plumas County
The stage from LaPorte to Oroville, California. **Taken:** $50 in gold nuggets, a silver watch and money from mail sacks.

7. October 2, 1878, Mendocino County
The Cahto to Ukiah, California, stage. **Taken:** $40 and mail sack contents.

8. October 3, 1878, Mendocino County
The stage from Covelo to Ukiah, California. **Taken:** Undisclosed amount.

9. June 21, 1879, Butte County
The Forbestown to Oroville, California, stage. **Taken:** Undisclosed amount.

10. October 25, 1879, Shasta County
A nighttime robbery on the Roseburg, Oregon, to Yreka-Redding, California, stage. **Taken:** Undisclosed amount from Wells Fargo and $1,400 from mail pouches.

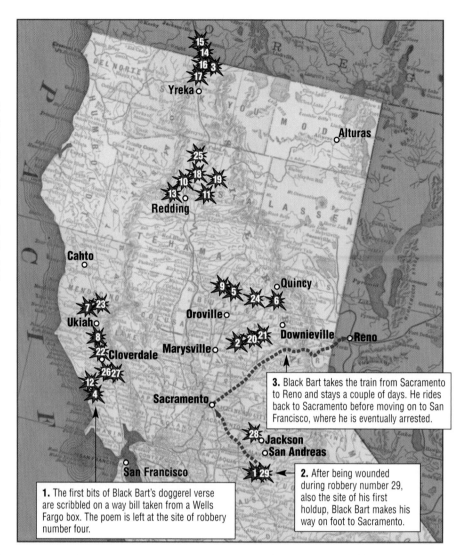

3. Black Bart takes the train from Sacramento to Reno and stays a couple of days. He rides back to Sacramento before moving on to San Francisco, where he is eventually arrested.

1. The first bits of Black Bart's doggerel verse are scribbled on a way bill taken from a Wells Fargo box. The poem is left at the site of robbery number four.

2. After being wounded during robbery number 29, also the site of his first holdup, Black Bart makes his way on foot to Sacramento.

A Close Shave

After walking from Copperopolis to Sacramento, Black Bart gets a shave and orders a new suit of clothes. In the 1950s, Arizona artist Lon Megargee memorialized this event in a famous painting commissioned by the A-1 Beer Company. (The painting is one of a series that the company reproduced as barroom posters.)

– TRUE WEST ARCHIVES –

11. October 27, 1879, Shasta County
The Alturas to Redding, California, stage. **Taken:** Undetermined.

12. July 22, 1880, Sonoma County
The stage from Point Arena to Duncan Mills, California. **Taken:** Undetermined amount. Whether the robber was Black Bart remains a point of contention to this day.

13. September 1, 1880, Shasta County
The Weaverville to Redding, California, stage. **Taken:** A little more than $100.

14. September 16, 1880, Jackson County, Oregon
The second nighttime robbery of the Roseburg, Oregon, to Yreka, California, stage, occurring one mile north of the state line. **Taken:** Approximately $1,000.

15. September 23, 1880, Jackson County, Oregon
The Roseburg, Oregon, to Redding, California, stage, robbed three miles north of the border. **Taken:** $1,000 in gold dust and from mail sack.

16. November 20, 1880, Siskiyou County
Again, the Roseburg, Oregon, to Redding, California, stage—a mile south of the state line shortly after dark. **Taken:** Unknown.

17. August 31, 1881, Siskiyou County
Around one a.m., the third robbery of the Roseburg, Oregon, to Yreka, California, stage. The stage is robbed 10 miles north of Yreka. **Taken:** Wells Fargo loss not disclosed.

18. October 8, 1881, Shasta County
Midnight robbery of the Yreka to Redding, California, stage near Bass Hill. **Taken:** $60.

19. October 11, 1881, Shasta County
The Alturas to Redding, California, stage stops at Montgomery Creek to make a harness repair and is robbed again. **Taken:** Undisclosed.

20. December 15, 1881, Yuba County
The Downieville to Marysville, California, stage. **Taken:** Wells Fargo reports "small loss."

21. December 27, 1881, Nevada County
The North San Juan to Smartsville, California, stage. **Taken:** Wells Fargo reports a small loss.

22. January 26, 1882, Mendocino County
The stage from Ukiah to Cloverdale, California. **Taken:** Unknown.

23. June 14, 1882, Mendocino County
The Willits to Ukiah, California, stage. **Taken:** Estimated $300 and mail sack contents.

24. July 13, 1882, Plumas County
Black Bart is foiled by shotgun blasts when he attempts to rob the LaPorte to Oroville, California, stage once more. (A buckshot pellet creases the robber's forehead, leaving a deep scar.)

25. September 17, 1882, Shasta County
The second robbery of the Yreka to Redding, California, stage at Bass Hill. **Taken:** Thirty-five cents from Wells Fargo.

26. November 23, 1882, Sonoma County
The Lakeport to Cloverdale, California, stage, robbed six miles from Cloverdale. **Taken:** $475 and several mail sacks.

27. April 12, 1883, Sonoma County
Again, the Lakeport to Cloverdale, California, stage. **Taken:** $32.50 and mail sack contents.

28. June 23, 1883, Amador County
The stage from Jackson to Lone, California. **Taken:** $750 and mail sack contents.

29. November 3, 1883, Calaveras County
The Sonora to Milton, California, stage is stopped at the site of the first Black Bart holdup in 1875. **Taken:** Possibly $4,764.

Legendary Poetry

Although Black Bart only leaves two poems at the scenes of his robberies, they contribute to his legendary fame. Some described them as "doggerel," but one thing is certain: He had an excellent sense of humor.

Here I lay me down to sleep
To wait the coming morrow
Perhaps success perhaps defeat
and everlasting sorrow.
Let come what will. I'll try it on
My condition can't be worse,
But if there's money on the box,
It's munny in my purse.

—BLACK BART, THE P o 8.

Where He Got the Name

The infamous robber refused to acknowledge that his real name was Charles E. Boles and served his prison term as Charles E. Bolton.

As for the nom de plume "Black Bart," Boles admitted he got the name from a character in William Henry Rhodes' "The Case of Summerfield," an 1871 serial that ran in the *Sacramento Union*. Boles admitted, "when I was casting around for a pseudonym, the name just popped into my head."

Wells Fargo Superintendent James B. Hume (left), along with Detective Harry Morse, grilled Boles for three hours, but the suspect didn't confess his guilt for some time.

– TRUE WEST ARCHIVES –

Aftermath: Odds & Ends

On November 17, 1883, Charles Bolton, alias Black Bart, pleaded guilty to a single charge of robbery and was sentenced to a remarkably light term of six years in San Quentin. With time off for good behavior, he was released after serving four years and two months.

The newspapers had a field day charging that Black Bart made a deal with the officers in exchange for the stolen gold. Harry Morse suffered the harshest criticism, as the papers questioned his version of the arrest and insisted that an informant had actually led Morse to Bart. One paper, *The San Francisco Examiner*, even questioned whether Boles was Bart.

Wells Fargo paid Morse and Calaveras County Sheriff Ben Thorn the bulk of the $800 reward. Then Thorn and Morse got into a public spat, accusing each other of malfeasance in the case. Thorn got the final salvo when he publicly reminded Morse of his bragging about an extra-marital affair during their ride from San Andreas to recover the stolen gold. It was a low blow from Thorn, but it worked. Morse never responded.

Black Bart was released from prison in January of 1888. By mid-year, he was back in the news after three more stage holdups, in which Black Bart was named by Jim Hume as the main suspect. Boles disappeared for good. Even his long suffering wife never heard from him again.

Recommended: *Black Bart: Boulevardier Bandit* by George Hoeper, published by Word Dancer Press; and *Lawman: The Life and Times of Harry Morse, 1835-1912* by John Boessenecker, published by University of Oklahoma Press.

Reason McConnell was driving a "mud wagon," like this one, on Funk Hill. It had wider wheels for better traction in the mountains and foothills of California and Oregon.

– TRUE WEST ARCHIVES –

LAY LADY GAY

BAT MASTERSON VS MELVIN KING

MOLLIE PROTECTS HER MAN

THREE DIFFERENT VERSIONS OF THE FIGHT

Mollie Brennan and Bat Masterson.

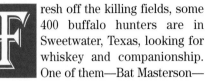

Fresh off the killing fields, some 400 buffalo hunters are in Sweetwater, Texas, looking for whiskey and companionship. One of them—Bat Masterson—has found both. He has hooked up with a popular lass, Mollie Brennan, at the Lady Gay, a theatre and dance hall saloon.

Unfortunately, Sgt. Melvin King has also taken a fancy to Mollie. When he hears about Bat making time with his girl, he heads to the Gay on the double, carrying a full head of steam, a bellyful of rotgut whiskey and a loaded six-gun.

At this point, the scant verified accounts begin to diverge dramatically. Here are the three versions of what happens next:

Version One

It is after hours, and Bat is in a room at the Lady Gay with Mollie.

Melvin pounds on the door. Thinking it is a friend wanting a nightcap, Bat unlocks the door.

Melvin lurches into the room with his pistol drawn. Seeing Mollie in bed, his worst suspicions are confirmed. He points his six-shooter at Bat and threatens to kill him. Shrieking at Melvin, Mollie jumps in front of Bat just as Melvin pulls the trigger. The bullet hits her in the stomach, angles through her body and strikes Bat in the pelvic region. As Mollie collapses, Bat staggers backwards and grabs his revolver. Bat fires, hitting Melvin in the heart and killing him instantly.

Version Two

Melvin enters the Lady Gay at the height of the evening's festivities. The saloon is jumping with soldiers, buffalo hunters, gamblers and soiled doves.

Seeing Bat dancing with Mollie, Melvin pulls his pistol and fires, hitting Mollie and Bat. Bat pulls his pistol and returns fire, killing Melvin.

Several of Melvin's friends pull their weaponry and attempt to get at Bat, who is lying seriously wounded on the dance floor.

Before they can get to Bat, gambler Ben Thompson leaps on a faro table with two drawn pistols and holds the troopers at bay until Bat can be moved to safer quarters.

Version Three

A gunfight breaks out inside the Lady Gay between buffalo hunters and soldiers. Two of the soldiers are wounded and one killed (Melvin), while one of the dance hall girls (Mollie) is killed. In this version, no mention is made of Bat's involvement or of his being shot.

In a jealous rage, Sgt. King lets loose with his pistol just as Mollie Brennan steps in front of Masterson (who is recoiling and reaching for his own weapon).

Bat Masterson

Ben Thompson

Sgt. Melvin King

Mollie Brennan

"[Ben Thompson] was absolutely without fear and his nerves were those of the finest steel. He shot at an adversary with the same precision and deliberation that he shot at a target."

—*Bat Masterson,* Human Life *magazine, 1907*

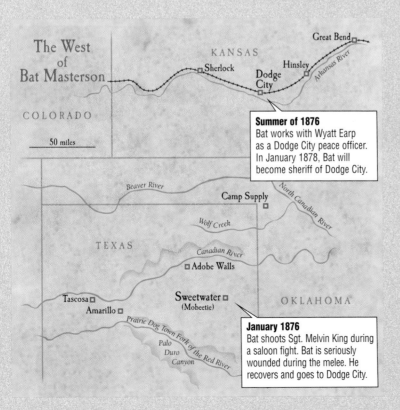

The West of Bat Masterson

KANSAS

Great Bend

Sherlock   Hinsley
Dodge
City

Arkansas River

COLORADO

50 miles

Summer of 1876
Bat works with Wyatt Earp as a Dodge City peace officer. In January 1878, Bat will become sheriff of Dodge City.

Beaver River

Camp Supply

North Canadian River

Wolf Creek

TEXAS

Canadian River

□ Adobe Walls

Tascosa □

Amarillo □

Sweetwater □
(Mobeetie)

OKLAHOMA

Prairie Dog Town Fork of the Red River

Palo
Duro
Canyon

January 1876
Bat shoots Sgt. Melvin King during a saloon fight. Bat is seriously wounded during the melee. He recovers and goes to Dodge City.

Aftermath: Odds & Ends

In Version One, the dance hall owner and several others heard the shots and rushed to the scene. A doctor was summoned, and he pronounced Bat Masterson's and Mollie Brennan's chances as nil. Mollie and Sgt. Melvin King soon died (although Version One has Melvin dying instantly, a newspaper account reports him being shot on Jan. 24 and dying on Jan. 25). Bat was taken to the nearby military encampment, where an army physician successfully removed the bullet from Bat's pelvis and nursed him back to health. Bat used a cane for the rest of his life.

⁕

Version One comes from Bat's younger brother, Thomas Masterson, Jr., who was 17 at the time of the incident. Interviewed in 1937, Tom claimed he heard the story from Bat when his older brother came home a few weeks after the incident.

⁕

Version Two comes from Wyatt Earp, who told his version of events to Stuart Lake (*Frontier Marshal*) in 1929. Earp didn't claim to be there.

⁕

It's interesting to note Ben Thompson knew Mollie very well, as she had been his brother Billy's girlfriend in Kansas. Bat Masterson biographer Robert K. DeArment wrote that if Thompson's role in the fight is true, it must have been the genesis of the friendship between Bat and the gambler. The two crossed paths again in Kansas, as did Wyatt Earp, and Bat rated Thompson the best of all the gunfighters (see quote at left).

⁕

Version Three is from the memoirs of George Curry, published in 1958. Curry, 14 in 1876, lived in Sweetwater at the time of the shooting.

⁕

Recommended: *Bat Masterson: The Man and the Legend* by Robert K. DeArment, published by University of Oklahoma Press.

WHAM, BAM, THANK YOU UNCLE SAM!

UNCLE SAM VS MORMON OUTLAWS

SPECTACULAR PAYROLL ROBBERY PULLED OFF WITH HALF A HITCH

"Look out, you black sons of bitches!"

MAY 11, 1889

United States Army Paymaster Maj. Joseph Washington Wham (rhymes with bomb) is riding in a dougherty (canopied ambulance), on his way to pay "all troops in the muster of April 30," which includes all the soldiers at Arizona's Forts Hauchuca, Bowie, Grant, Thomas and Apache, and San Carlos (see map, opposite page).

Having successfully paid the troopers at Forts Bowie and Grant, Wham and his Buffalo Soldier escort are on their way to Fort Thomas, around the mountain from Grant.

Private Hamilton Lewis drives Maj. Wham's lead wagon, carrying Wham, his clerk William Gibbon, mule tender Pvt. Caldwell and Sgt. Benjamin Brown, as well as a strongbox full of mostly gold coins, valued at just over $28,000. A second wagon follows Wham's with an armed escort of 10 Buffalo Soldiers stationed at Fort Grant.

As both wagons enter a narrow defile known as Bloody Run (named for an Apache attack on this spot seven years earlier), the driver of the advance wagon spies a good sized boulder in the center of the road.

Gibbon and several soldiers get out to investigate. As they walk forward, one of them remarks, "That rock was rolled there by hand."

Gibbon reaches down to throw a smaller rock off the road when a voice is heard from above: "Look out, you black sons of bitches!" The outlaw, dressed in buckskin, fires his pistols, a signal that

unleashes a volley of rifle fire from the ridge, bringing down the lead mule on Wham's wagon and two mules on the escort wagon. The soldiers retrieve their rifles (stored unloaded in the bed of the second wagon) as the terrified mules buck and pull at their traces, dragging both wagons off the road and into the rocks.

Rifles fire from both sides of the road as Maj. Wham directs his troops to find cover. Multiple shooters rain bullets down at the exposed troopers: Pvt. Lewis takes a bullet in the gut; Pvt. Squire Williams is hit in the ankle; and Sgt. Brown is struck in the arm and side. The troopers take up a position behind a small ledge, but the attackers command the heights and rain a withering fire at them, striking several more troopers. Finally, several of the soldiers begin to fire back, but they can't hold the position and retreat down a ravine draining into Cottonwood Wash. Major Wham joins them as they are driven to the creek bottom, about 300 yards from the wagons. With wounded troopers lying all around him, Wham has given up defending the payroll.

Several robbers come down from the fortifications and climb into Wham's wagon. The troopers hear violent hammering (they can't see the wagon). The soldiers count 12 to 15 men making their way back up and over the ridge where the attack commenced. The fight has lasted about two hours, but the attackers have achieved their goal and the payroll is gone.

A dozen guns let loose a sharp volley of fire, setting off a commotion among the men and mules of Wham's party. That's Frankie Campbell down the road from the boulder, just about to be unhorsed.

The Wham Robbery

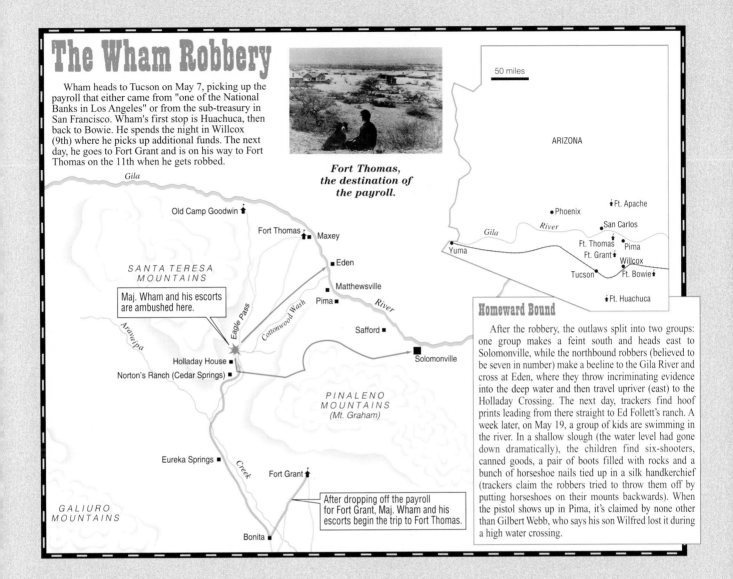

Wham heads to Tucson on May 7, picking up the payroll that either came from "one of the National Banks in Los Angeles" or from the sub-treasury in San Francisco. Wham's first stop is Huachuca, then back to Bowie. He spends the night in Willcox (9th) where he picks up additional funds. The next day, he goes to Fort Grant and is on his way to Fort Thomas on the 11th when he gets robbed.

Fort Thomas, the destination of the payroll.

50 miles

ARIZONA

Ft. Apache
Phoenix
San Carlos
Gila   River
Ft. Thomas   Pima
Yuma   Ft. Grant
Willcox
Tucson   Ft. Bowie
Ft. Huachuca

Gila

Old Camp Goodwin

Fort Thomas   Maxey

SANTA TERESA MOUNTAINS

Eden

Matthewsville

Maj. Wham and his escorts are ambushed here.

Pima   River

Safford

Eagle Pass

Cottonwood Wash

Aravaipa

Holladay House

Solomonville

Norton's Ranch (Cedar Springs)

PINALENO MOUNTAINS (Mt. Graham)

Eureka Springs   Creek

Fort Grant

After dropping off the payroll for Fort Grant, Maj. Wham and his escorts begin the trip to Fort Thomas.

GALIURO MOUNTAINS

Bonita

Homeward Bound

After the robbery, the outlaws split into two groups: one group makes a feint south and heads east to Solomonville, while the northbound robbers (believed to be seven in number) make a beeline to the Gila River and cross at Eden, where they throw incriminating evidence into the deep water and then travel upriver (east) to the Holladay Crossing. The next day, trackers find hoof prints leading from there straight to Ed Follett's ranch. A week later, on May 19, a group of kids are swimming in the river. In a shallow slough (the water level had gone down dramatically), the children find six-shooters, canned goods, a pair of boots filled with rocks and a bunch of horseshoe nails tied up in a silk handkerchief (trackers claim the robbers tried to throw them off by putting horseshoes on their mounts backwards). When the pistol shows up in Pima, it's claimed by none other than Gilbert Webb, who says his son Wilfred lost it during a high water crossing.

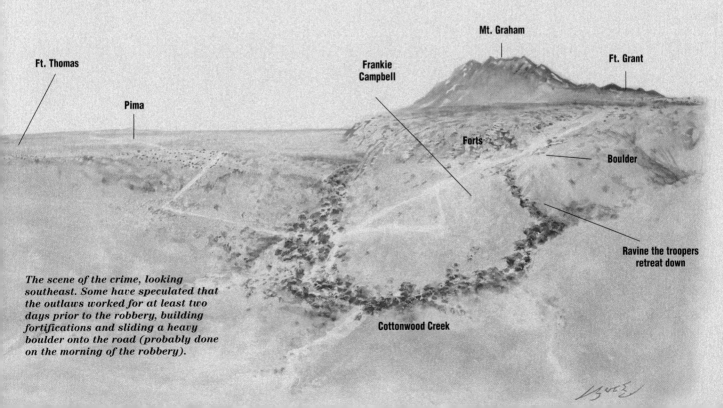

Ft. Thomas

Pima

Mt. Graham

Frankie Campbell

Ft. Grant

Forts

Boulder

Ravine the troopers retreat down

Cottonwood Creek

The scene of the crime, looking southeast. Some have speculated that the outlaws worked for at least two days prior to the robbery, building fortifications and sliding a heavy boulder onto the road (probably done on the morning of the robbery).

The Suspects

William Ellison Beck, a.k.a. "Cyclone Bill," a former Texan with a bad leg (jokesters claim he stands "5'6" on one foot and 6'2" on the other"); arrested in a Clifton saloon on May 15. Bill got his nickname after absconding with a Yuma freight wagon. When cornered in Tucson, he claimed a desert cyclone swept up him and the wagon and dropped them both in the Old Pueblo. Recently, Cochise County Sheriff Texas John Slaughter ran him out of Tombstone.

Marcus E. Cunningham, a.k.a. "the Bull Baron of the Bonita," a New Yorker who came to Arizona to work on the Southern Pacific railroad; arrested at Fort Thomas by Deputy Marshal Billy Breakenridge and others on May 16. Marcus ran a saloon and butcher shop in Maxey, worked as a ranch foreman and served as election inspector and deputy sheriff. He also campaigned unsuccessfully as the democratic nominee for sheriff in 1888.

Lyman Follett, a rancher who had been previously arrested with Cunningham for stealing government livestock; arrested on May 20. During the fight, one of the robbers was wounded in the hand; after the robbery, Lyman had an injured hand. Four days later, his three brothers, **Warren** (**Wall**), **Joseph Edward** (**Ed**) and **William**, were held at the Fort Thomas guardhouse (William was released on May 27 for lack of evidence).

Wilfred Webb, a rancher; arrested on May 24 as he drove his wagon up to his home in Pima. Wilfred's father, Gilbert, was in Tucson at the time, allegedly on business, but he aroused suspicion by helping Cunningham make bail. Gilbert was arrested on June 2, at the San Xavier Hotel, next to the train station, for "meddling with federal prisoners and witnesses."

David Mayer Rogers, a cowhand for the Webb Cattle Company, gave himself up at Fort Thomas on May 25, the same day **Sebird H. "Bud" Henderson**, a Pima farmer and friend of the Folletts, was arrested by a 10th Cavalry detachment in Globe. The next day, another cowhand who worked for Webb, **Thomas Norman Lamb**, was served papers at his home in Matthewsville.

Cyclone Bill

Wilfred (W.T.) Webb

Sheriff Marshall

Thomas Lamb

Ed Follett

Mark Cunningham

Andrew Carlson

David Rogers

Also Suspected, But Never Charged:

Sheriff **"Shef" Marshall** (moved to Utah shortly after the robbery); **Jacob Felshaw**; **Joseph Foster, Jr.** (a brother-in-law of the Follett brothers); **Abe Winsor** (a saloonkeeper in Pima); **Andrew Carlson**; **William E. "Doc" Dowdie**; **Buck Tyson**; **William Forbes**; **John Dowdle**; and just about every other person who lived along the Gila at the time of the robbery.

Robber Fort #1   Cottonwood Creek   Ravine

The most famous photo of the Wham Robbery site, taken the day after the robbery by an army photographer. The main robber fortification is near the cedar tree, the dead mule from the first wagon is still where he died (see red circle) and the ravine where the soldiers fled is at far right.

The Man with the Plan

Gilbert Webb (center), 52, served his Mormon mission in Hawaii, had three wives in Utah, got crossways with Brigham Young after failing to deliver on a contract to supply telegraph poles, declared bankruptcy and skated on the intervention of his attractive sister, Ann Eliza, who agreed to marry Young in exchange for retiring her brother's debt. Webb moved to Arizona to help grade track for the Atlantic & Pacific Railroad and later landed in the Gila River community of Pima where he started several businesses, including a store, a real estate operation, a stage line from Solomonville to the rail head at Willcox and the Webb Cattle Company. He also served on the town's first city council and as mayor, and helped build Pima's first school.

A year prior to the robbery, Webb's name was struck from the Pima Mormon rolls for his alleged illicit affair with a widow (although he still chaired the church's building committee). At the time of the robbery, Webb was on the verge of bankruptcy; his stage line and his store had been shut down, and he didn't have the capital to fulfill several lucrative government contracts. Many people in town owed him money. The need for capital was clear, and the means was on its way—being carried by Wham's wagon.

Righteous Robbers

By most accounts, the Wham Payroll Robbery is almost a community project, led by Pima's mayor and major job provider Gilbert Webb, who convinces most of the cowboys and farmers to participate by pinning the survival of the town (and by extension, his fellow Mormon citizens) on liberating U.S. funds. It isn't a hard sell because the U.S. government has been harassing Mormons for a long time. The gang of 12-15 includes Webb's three sons: Wilfred (who, at the time of the holdup, is facing an indictment for stealing cattle), Leslie and Milo.

The robbers do not wear masks, probably because masks would imply wrongdoing. Webb & Associates likely rationalize that the black troopers are cursed and unworthy of the money. At that time, a virulent strain of Mormonism contends that blacks are descendants from Cain, who was cursed by God, and that his descendants' dark-colored skin is the "mark of Cain" (many who believe this also apply it to Indians). By liberating much needed capital for the work of God, from an evil government protected by descendants of Cain, the robbers may not have felt the need to wear masks.

A local quote from that time says it all: "The nigger soldiers would just waste the money on liquor, gambling, and whores, so why not take it and use it to the benefit of a community that really needed some cash to stave off bankruptcy for Webb and some of his neighbors."

A Pima pioneer, Don Pace, later claims that "the Pima colony would have been starved out if not for the ingenuity of Gilbert Webb."

The ridgeline along Bloody Run explodes with rifle fire. Army investigators later find numerous "forts" along the escarpment.

The Eyewitness in the Bright Yellow Blouse

Riding a big bay, Frankie Campbell, a.k.a. Frankie Stratton, is decked out in a bright yellow, tight-waisted blouse, a billowing wine-colored skirt and a large floppy straw hat decorated with a red paper rose and red velvet streamers.

Her husband is locked up in the Fort Grant guardhouse, accused of killing a fellow soldier. The couple are known gamblers (some speculate Frankie is a soiled dove), and they have at least one child. Frankie insists on riding with the paymaster entourage to Fort Thomas to collect on gambling debts on payday.

Riding just ahead of the wagons, Frankie is beyond the boulder when the shooting starts and startles her horse, who throws her off. She takes cover under a bush, near the fork in the road leading to Cottonwood Creek, and witnesses the battle with a ringside seat. After the robbers leave, she approaches the troops. Major Wham arrests her on suspicion of being in collusion with the outlaws. She is left behind with the severely wounded while Wham commandeers the escort and heads for Fort Thomas.

At the subsequent trial, Frankie keeps the jurors in stitches with her humorous responses.

The Wounded, the Brave and the Not So Brave

Sgt. Ben Brown, arm and side

Hamilton Lewis, side

Squire Williams, leg

George Arrington, shoulder

James Wheeler, arm

Benjamin Burge, leg and arm

Thomas Hams, arm

Julius Harrison, ear

The robbers think the Buffalo Soldiers will run at the first salvo, but although a couple do flee the scene, Cpl. Isaiah Mays (below) and Sgt. Ben Brown put up a stiff resistance, both receiving the Medal of Honor for their bravery.

Not Everyone Fights

Private Caldwell (recently discharged and hitching a ride) runs for it. "He uses his limbs pretty swift for an old man," Frankie Campbell remarks about Caldwell at the trial. Private Fox takes cover behind the ledge but doesn't fire back at the robbers. One of the folk tales of the fight is that Frankie Campbell places a shawl around Fox's neck and tells him not to remove it, and he is spared because of it.

Corporal Isaiah Mays bravely returns fire at Fort #1 as incoming rounds rake the four-foot ridge Wham and his men have taken refuge behind. The robbers have a fort south of the ridge (see right), and their leader, Gilbert Webb, also sends more shooters across the road to flank the soldiers' position.

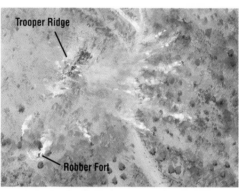

Trooper Ridge

Robber Fort

How to Spot the Real Robbers

Mastermind Gilbert Webb (seated, center, with cane) hires the best attorneys that stolen money can buy (a reported $10,000 of the robbery loot goes to pay them), but he suffers from the old gypsy curse: May you be found among lawyers. They are: Marcus Smith (7), Ben Goodrich (8), Ben and Frank Hereford (10 and 11). Although they successfully dodge the law, Webb cowboys David Rogers and Thomas Lamb (3 and 4) never see a dime from the robbery. The Follett brothers, Lyman and Ed (1 and 2) and Wall (5) allegedly receive $3,000 each, as does one of the only non-Mormons in on the heist, Marcus Cunningham (6). Gilbert's son Wilfred (12) ends up owning the 76 Ranch, which encompasses Mount Graham. He also has a very successful political career in Arizona where rogues and thieves have long prospered.

Aftermath: Odds & Ends

After a marathon trial in Tucson involving major politics and infighting (the original judge was removed), all seven defendants were acquitted. But even though an all-white jury exonerated the accused men, local kids yelled epithets at the men ("Damn Mormon Robbers!") when they boarded the train for home.

⸺ ☆ ⸺

Gilbert Webb allegedly took most of the money from the robbery to pay off his massive debts, forgive debts to fellow Pimans (especially those who helped pull off the robbery) and pay for the attorneys. The next year, Webb was elected a delegate to the Territorial Democratic Convention, but then he was indicted for defrauding the Pima school district of $160. He left Pima in 1891 and ended up taking a railroad job in New Mexico. Eventually moving to Colonia Juárez, Mexico, he died and was buried there in 1923—a year after the Mormon Church had reinstated him.

⸺ ☆ ⸺

Medal of Honor recipients Benjamin Brown and Isaiah Mays stayed in the army, with Brown retiring in 1904 and dying six years later. Suffering from rheumatism, Mays resigned from the army in 1893 and spent the rest of his life around Bonita, just outside Fort Grant. He tried for years to get an army pension but failed, dying at Phoenix's Arizona State Hospital in 1925. (Buried in the hospital's cemetery, his body was rediscovered in the late 1960s and a proper headstone was erected.)

⸺ ☆ ⸺

Gilbert Webb's attractive sister, Ann Eliza, who got him out of hot water in Salt Lake, divorced Brigham Young in 1875 and gained nationwide notoriety as the author of *Wife No. 19, or the Story of a Life in Bondage.*

⸺ ☆ ⸺

Recommended: *Ambush at Bloody Run: The Wham Paymaster Robbery of 1889* by Larry D. Ball, published by Arizona Historical Society.

ADAIR BEFORE THEY DIE

THE DALTON GANG VS KATY RAILROAD GUARDS

THE LAST SUCCESSFUL RAID OF THE DALTONS TURNS TRAGIC

The Dalton Gang's triumph is short-lived.

JULY 15, 1892

Dead Men Riding

Eight outlaws ride towards Adair, Oklahoma. In addition to their daredevil ways, each share one commonality: All of them will stop a hail of bullets (see p.27), but only one will live to tell about it. The robbers are believed to have been Bob, Grat (just escaped from jail in California) and Emmett Dalton, Bill Doolin, Bill Power, Dick Broadwell, Charley Pierce and Bitter Creek Newcomb.

iding eight strong, the Dalton Gang enters Adair, Indian Territory (present-day Oklahoma). They commandeer the train station, preparing to pilfer Katy Train No. 2 (a Missouri, Kansas & Texas passenger train). When the train glides into the station at 9:42 p.m., the gang boards, capturing members of the train crew without incident and telling them to obey or "have their brains blown out."

As the crew is marched down to the express car, one of the gang members begins shooting towards the town, evidently trying to discourage towns-people from getting any ideas about joining the party.

After some resistance, the outlaws break into the express car and force the

One of the outlaws, probably Bob Dalton, sends a withering fire into the coal shed where the railroad guards have forted up. Accurate, pinpoint firing knocks them out of the fight.

fireman and the messenger to open the through safe (which contains little loot). The gang then rifles through the car and loads the collected money into a stolen spring wagon. (Although the exact amount taken is unknown, most historians estimate the take at about $17,000.)

As the robbers load up, Winchester slugs begin whipping very close to the heads of the outlaws. Eight train guards, including lawmen J.J. Kinney and Capt. J.H. LeFlore, are shooting out the windows of the smoking car and at the gang.

With the firing increasing, the lawmen get off the train and "fort up" in a coal house next to the tracks. The lawmen pour a heavy fire at the crowd around the express car. The robbers use their hostages as shields while they shoot into the wood building.

Within moments, three of the lawmen inside are hit and knocked out of the fight. The July 21 *Indian Chieftain* reported the casualties, "A bullet went through the flesh of Mr. Kinney's shoulder, another struck Johnson's watch and imbedded itself in his arm, while Charley Leflore *[sic]* had the stock of his gun struck with a shot and the slivers driven into his arm."

Gang member Charley Pierce finally shows up with the horses. While one outlaw returns fire at the guards, the others mount up and clatter down the streets of the small town, sending about 20 shots at two men sitting in front of

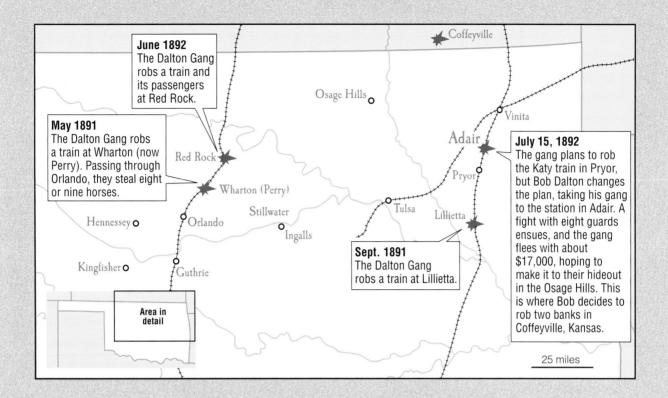

June 1892
The Dalton Gang robs a train and its passengers at Red Rock.

May 1891
The Dalton Gang robs a train at Wharton (now Perry). Passing through Orlando, they steal eight or nine horses.

Coffeyville

Osage Hills

Vinita

Adair

Pryor

Red Rock

Wharton (Perry)

Stillwater

Tulsa

Lillietta

Hennessey

Orlando

Ingalls

Kingfisher

Guthrie

July 15, 1892
The gang plans to rob the Katy train in Pryor, but Bob Dalton changes the plan, taking his gang to the station in Adair. A fight with eight guards ensues, and the gang flees with about $17,000, hoping to make it to their hideout in the Osage Hills. This is where Bob decides to rob two banks in Coffeyville, Kansas.

Sept. 1891
The Dalton Gang robs a train at Lillietta.

Area in detail

25 miles

As the gang rides through the town after the robbery, one or more of the members fire shots at bystanders. The promiscuous bullets strike two doctors. With the subsequent death of one of them, Dr. Goff (he lived for three days), rewards for the gang reach $40,000.

the Skinner Drug Store. Both bystanders are doctors—Dr. W.L. Goff is mortally wounded; Dr. T.S. Youngblood will lose part of his right foot. (Gang apologists later claim the two men were shot by errant bullets fired by the train guards, yet it is more likely the men were hit by outlaw bullets.)

The gang's last successful raid is over, but their lawless run is rapidly coming to a violent end.

Deadly Daltons' Deadhead

After a flurry of robberies in the Indian Territory (see map, above), Bob Dalton and his gang planned on hitting Red Rock Station. When the gang got into position at 10:30 p.m. on June 1, Bob didn't like the look of the darkened smoking car as the train pulled into the small, one-horse station.

Bob sensed that the train carried a car full of loaded Winchesters. Bob's suspicion turned out to be correct. Inside were Wells Fargo detective Fred Dodge and the formidable U.S. Deputy Marshal Heck Thomas, among others.

Letting that train depart, the gang stood by. Soon enough, an unescorted express train arrived, and the gang moved in for the kill. When the gang strong-armed their way into the car, they unfortunately found little money. The big money had gone through with the first train. The chagrined gang took what was there (less than $3,000) and then mugged a train employee of his gold watch and pocket cash, and,

probably just for spite, took the crew's lunchboxes.

The gang scattered to confuse pursuit but regrouped at one of their favorite caves, supposedly near Tulsa. There, they discussed raiding the Katy Train at Pryor Creek. But Bob, who noticed an Indian farmer had spotted them and worried the man would alert the authorities, thought it'd be wise to hit the Katy train at the Adair station instead. The others agreed.

Although the raid in Adair would end up a success, time was running out for the gang.

Bob and Grat Dalton

"Nemesis" is what Emmett Dalton called Deputy Marshal Heck Thomas (seated front row, at left). Many believe Thomas' dogged pursuit caused Emmett's brother Bob to attack Coffeyville hastily and contributed directly to the gang's demise. Wells Fargo certainly agreed: "We feel that your work, more than anything, brought about the extermination of this gang ... and are happy to hand you, from our railway and express pool, a check herewith in the amount of $1,500."

Pawnee Gallery,

'ISS NORA HANSON,

Pawnee, O. T.

The Best in the Business

By the time of the train robbery in Adair, the Daltons are already being chased by some of the best lawmen in the business, including Wells Fargo Detective Fred Dodge and Deputy Marshals Heck Thomas and Chris Madsen.

J.J. Kinney, special detective of the railroad, and Capt. J.H. LeFlore, chief of the Cherokee Indian Police, discover the Daltons, by chance, when the gang members board the Adair train.

On July 21, 1892, the *Indian Chieftain* reported the robbery, stating that once the guards became aware of the robbery, they opened fire at the outlaws through the car windows; the robbers responded in kind.

The article also stated, "The railroad and express companies have joined in an offer of $5,000 each 'for conviction, the aggregate sum not to exceed $40,000.' Under these terms there will be no pursuit by men of experience in the country. Those who know the Dalton boys, and there can be no doubt but that they were in this hold-up *[sic]*, know they cannot be captured alive. To kill them does not comply with the terms and will not secure the reward but it will expose whoever does to prosecution in the U.S. Court in Fort Smith."

And Then There Were Five

With several posses less than 24 hours behind and closing in, Bob Dalton makes a hasty plan and the gang heads north to Coffeyville, Kansas. On this raid, there are only five members—the three Dalton brothers, Bill Power and Dick Broadwell.

Not invited, or perhaps declining, are outlaw stalwarts Bill Doolin, Bitter Creek Newcomb and Charley Pierce. Some believe Doolin actually does go along but drops out at the last minute because his horse comes up lame or perhaps he has a brief moment of clarity. Others speculate Bob wants all the glory for the outrageous double heist (besides, the split would be sweeter). In any case, the other members of the so-called Doolin-Dalton Gang do not have long to run.

And then there were five.

(Not Shown: Charley Pierce, who is killed with Newcomb in 1895, see p. 48.)

W. B. Dougherty,
GUTHRIE, O. T.
Oklahoma Ave.,

Four years after the members of the so-called Doolin-Dalton Gang go down in a hail of bullets in Coffeyville, Bill Doolin (above) is peppered with deadly buckshot. (Not Shown: Charley Pierce, who is killed with Newcomb in 1895, see p. 48.)

Power

Grat D.

Newcomb

Emmett D.   **Broadwell**   **Bob D.**

Aftermath: Odds & Ends

From their hideout near Tulsa, the Daltons, along with Bill Power and Dick Broadwell, headed for their historic, and disastrous, fate in Coffeyville, Kansas, where they tried to rob two banks (see *Classic Gunfights Vol. I*).

The only survivor, Emmett Dalton (bottom of page), served 14 years and lived out his life in California where he became somewhat of a celebrity. The rest of the gang met a more grisly end (see scorecard at left).

(From left) Bill Power, Bob Dalton, Grat Dalton and Dick Broadwell.

Recommended: *Daltons! The Raid on Coffeyville, Kansas* by Robert Barr Smith, published by University of Oklahoma Press; *Shoot from the Lip* by Nancy B. Samuelson, published by Shooting Star Press; and *Captain Jack and the Dalton Gang* by John J. Kinney, published by University Press of Kansas

Emmett Dalton

How Did Davy Really Die?

Davy Crockett vs Santa Anna's Army

Did He Go Down Swinging?

You and What Army?

Crockett faces his attackers with the courage of a lion.

MARCH 6, 1836

Just after midnight, Gen. Santa Anna orders his 2,064 troops to move towards their assault positions. Select *Soldados* (soldiers) stealthily sneak up on Tejano sentries, who lie in dugouts positioned away from the Alamo, and slit the guards' throats.

Just before sunrise (around 5 a.m.) a *soldado* from the second column yells out "Viva Santa Anna!" His comrades echo the cry. Furious that he has lost the element of surprise, Santa Anna orders his musicians to sound the attack. A rocket battery fires the signal.

Four Mexican columns surge out of the darkness toward the shadowed walls of the Alamo. Awakened by the shouts, the Texans quickly man their cannons and commence a furious enfilade fire from the church and corral batteries, forcing the attackers coming in from the east to move north.

Musket and cannon fire pour from the walls of the Alamo, and three attacking columns stall at the north wall. The Texans are holding their own and laying down a deadly fire.

Momentum lost, Santa Anna commits his reserves. *Grenidiers* (grenediers) and *zapadores* (sappers) charge into the fight and finally succeed in breaching the Texan defense. Meanwhile, the *caballeria* (cavalry) breaches the Alamo's southwest corner from the west side. The Texans fighting there are quickly overwhelmed and fall back, taking refuge in the adobe apartments, convent and church. Mexican troops pour into the compound unchecked; others seize the abandoned batteries, turn them around and fire at the retreating Texans with their own cannons.

Hand-to-hand combat is fierce. The fighting turns especially bloody as the Mexican troops go room to room, overwhelming each pocket of resistance and shooting and bayoneting everything that moves.

Some 60 defenders break out of the Alamo heading east on Gonzales Road, but Santa Anna's cavalry is waiting and cuts them down.

An hour after the initial attack, Davy Crockett stands alone, still proudly and tenaciously defending his diminished position (see map, opposite page). A frightful gash angles across his forehead. Holding the barrel of his shattered rifle in his right hand and a Bowie knife dripping with blood in his left, Crockett faces his attackers with the courage of a lion. Twenty dead or dying Mexicans lie beneath his buckskin-clad feet.

The man from Tennessee crouches, daring his attackers to take him. As they move in for the kill, Davy swings wildly until he finally falls, fighting like a tiger until his last dying breath. The fight is over.

Well, not exactly

That's how we in the U.S. celebrated the death of the "King of the Wild Frontier" for a good part of the 20th century. Exemplifying the Texas creed that you have no business telling a story unless you can improve it, Davy's death scenario grew each time the story was retold.

Then, in 1955, at the height of the Disney Davy's fame, a diary from Mexico surfaced, claiming Davy had surrendered. For a long time, historians belittled and rebuked José Enrique de la Peña's diary. When they finally looked closely at the corroborating evidence, Davy's dramatic final scene began to change.

Let's take a look at the historical record:

Anglo Accounts

One of the first official reports of the Alamo fight comes from Gen. Sam Houston, writing to the commander at Goliad, March 11, 1836: "After the fort was carried, seven men surrendered and called for Santa Anna and quarter. They were murdered by his order."

Houston doesn't name Crockett, but his report reveals that from the beginning officials knew that a group of Alamo defenders had surrendered.

Here's a condensed version of one of the first news reports, appearing in the *Morning Courier & New-York Enquirer* on July 9, 1836:

"Six Americans were discovered near the wall yet unconquered. They were surrounded and ordered by General Castrillón to surrender, which they did under a promise of protection."

One of the six stepped forward with "a bold demeanor." The troops noticed his

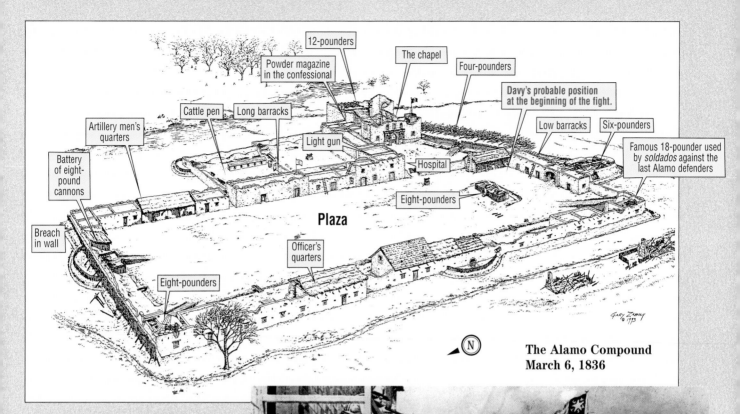

The Alamo Compound
March 6, 1836

Labels (clockwise):
12-pounders
Powder magazine in the confessional
The chapel
Four-pounders
Davy's probable position at the beginning of the fight.
Low barracks
Six-pounders
Famous 18-pounder used by *soldados* against the last Alamo defenders
Cattle pen
Long barracks
Light gun
Hospital
Eight-pounders
Artillery men's quarters
Battery of eight-pound cannons
Breach in wall
Eight-pounders
Officer's quarters
Plaza
N

"firmness and his noble bearing." An undaunted "David Crockett" boldly faced Gen. Santa Anna, looking him "steadfastly in the face."

"Sir, here are six prisoners I have taken alive; how shall I dispose of them?" Manuel Fernandez asked his commander.

Santa Anna fiercely looked at Castrillón, replying, "Have I not told you before how to dispose of them? Why do you bring them to me?"

Several junior officers pulled their swords and lunged at Crockett and the others, plunging their swords into "the bosoms of their defenseless prisoners."

Mexican Accounts

Ramón Martínez Caro, Santa Anna's personal secretary, reports in an 1837 pamphlet published in Mexico that "there were five who were discovered by General Castrillón while the soldiers stepped out of their ranks and set upon the prisoners until they were all killed."

De la Peña's diary offers a somewhat different account: "some seven men had survived the general carnage and, under the protection of General Castrillón, they were brought before Santa Anna. Among them ... was the naturalist David Crockett, well known in North America for his unusual adventures ... Santa Anna answered Castrillón's intervention

Davy Crockett fights to the end, while James Bowie (to his left) lies on a pallet.

– Courtesy Paul Hutton –

in Crockett's behalf with a gesture of indignation and, addressing himself to ... the troops closest to him, ordered his execution. The commanders and officers were outraged at this action and did not support the order ... but several officers who were around the president and who, perhaps, had not been present during the moment of danger ... thrust themselves forward ... and with swords in hand, fell upon these unfortunate, defenseless men just as a tiger leaps upon his prey. Though tortured before they were killed, these unfortunates died without complaining and without humiliating themselves before their torturers."

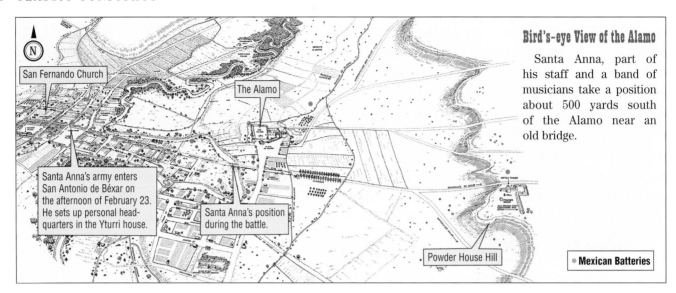

Bird's-eye View of the Alamo

Santa Anna, part of his staff and a band of musicians take a position about 500 yards south of the Alamo near an old bridge.

San Fernando Church

The Alamo

Santa Anna's army enters San Antonio de Béxar on the afternoon of February 23. He sets up personal head-quarters in the Yturri house.

Santa Anna's position during the battle.

Powder House Hill

• **Mexican Batteries**

The Breakthrough

Mexican forces attack the west wall, breaking through the posterns and windows, and climb over the walls. The north column assaults the wooden outerworks at the north wall, meeting fierce resistance. Santa Anna sends in reserves. With flanks exposed, the Texans defending the north wall abandon it and seek shelter in the long barracks and other houses within the compound. Mexican soldiers now pour into the unchecked Alamo from almost every direction. In the barracks and chapel, the surviving Texans brace themselves for their last brutal stand.

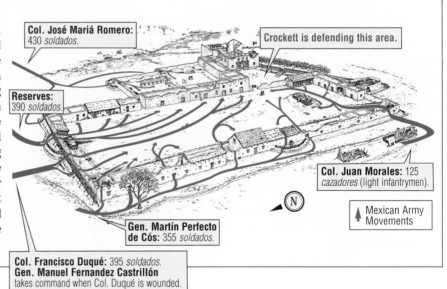

Col. José Mariá Romero: 430 *soldados.*

Crockett is defending this area.

Reserves: 390 *soldados.*

Col. Juan Morales: 125 *cazadores* (light infantrymen).

Gen. Martín Perfecto de Cós: 355 *soldados.*

Col. Francisco Duqué: 395 *soldados.*
Gen. Manuel Fernandez Castrillón takes command when Col. Duqué is wounded.

Mexican Army Movements

Fallen Defenders

Locations of where the defenders fell are based on:

- Research of Charles J. Long, a longtime curator of the Alamo
- Diary of José Enrique de la Peña
- Report of Francisco Ruiz, *alcalde* (mayor) of San Antonio at the time of the battle
- Citizen accounts by Susannah Dickinson and Amelia Williams

Dickinson's account of where Crockett fell coincides with the belief he went down swinging, while some historians believe that he was executed near the west wall.

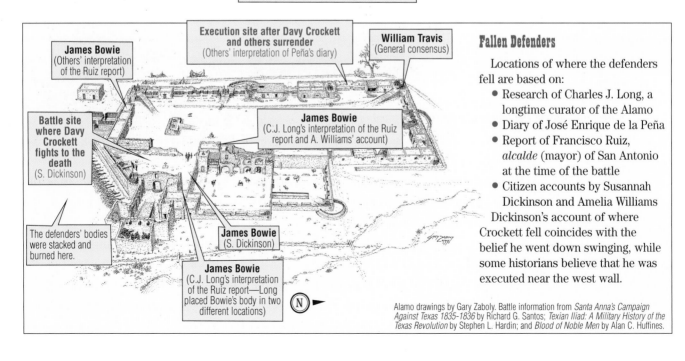

James Bowie (Others' interpretation of the Ruiz report)

Execution site after Davy Crockett and others surrender (Others' interpretation of Peña's diary)

William Travis (General consensus)

Battle site where Davy Crockett fights to the death (S. Dickinson)

James Bowie (C.J. Long's interpretation of the Ruiz report and A. Williams' account)

The defenders' bodies were stacked and burned here.

James Bowie (S. Dickinson)

James Bowie (C.J. Long's interpretation of the Ruiz report—Long placed Bowie's body in two different locations)

Alamo drawings by Gary Zaboly. Battle information from *Santa Anna's Campaign Against Texas 1835-1836* by Richard G. Santos; *Texian Iliad: A Military History of the Texas Revolution* by Stephen L. Hardin; and *Blood of Noble Men* by Alan C. Huffines.

This 1834 print of David Crockett is based on a lost oil painting by Samuel Osgood.

– Courtesy David Zucker –

This 19th-century etching of Gen. Antonio López de Santa Anna is based on a circa 1850 daguerreotype.

– Courtesy Paul Hutton –

The earliest known photograph of the Alamo is this daguerreotype. It was taken prior to 1850, which was when the U.S. Army repaired the Alamo and added the famous hump to the chapel (see below).

– Courtesy of the Center for American History, University of Texas at Austin; Below, True West Archives –

Aftermath: Odds & Ends

Although the Davy Crockett surrender scenario remains contentious, especially in Texas, author Dan Kilgore concludes, "Four officers and a sergeant—all of whom participated in the assault and observed the final tragedy—specifically identified Crockett as one of the captives.... Their accounts have come to light over a long period of time, several having surfaced only recently. Any one of them, standing alone, could be subject to question, but considered as a whole, the statements provide stronger documentation than can be claimed for any other incident during the battle."

Others believe Davy didn't even die at the Alamo. In 1840, William White's letter, printed in the *Austin City Gazette*, reported a visit to Guadalajara, Mexico, where a native stated a Texas prisoner had been forced to work in a mine. The enslaved miner was, of course, Davy Crockett. White claimed that Crockett wrote a letter to his family in Tennessee and had asked White to mail it for him. Even though the letter never arrived, Davy's son, John Crockett (a congressman from Tennessee) allegedly went to Mexico to search for his father.

"Too much has been made over the details of how David died at the Alamo. Such details are not important. What is important is that he died as he had lived. His life was one of indomitable bravery; his death was a death of intrepid courage. His life was one of wholehearted dedication to his concepts of liberty. He died staking his life against what he regarded as intolerable tyranny," wrote James A. Shackford in his 1956 book, *David Crockett*.

Recommended: *How Did Davy Die?* by Dan Kilgore, published by Texas A&M University Press; and *Eyewitness to the Alamo* by Bill Groneman, published by Republic of Texas Press.

I Shot the Sheriff
(And I Killed a Deputy, Too)

Billy the Kid and His Regulators vs Sheriff Brady and His Deputies

Heavy rain the night before leaves the ground soggy. The lawmen, armed with repeating rifles, sidestep the bogs as they walk down the main street of Lincoln, New Mexico.

APRIL 1, 1878

After eating breakfast at the Wortley Hotel in Lincoln, New Mexico, Sheriff William Brady walks out on the main street to meet his deputies: George Hindman, Jacob "Billy" Mathews, John Long (a.k.a. Frank Rivers) and George W. Peppin. It's approximately 9:00 in the morning.

A heavy rain has drenched the Bonito River Valley. The formidable men walk east down the center of the muddy street, picking their way around the bogs.

As the quintet passes the Ham Mills residence (see map, p. 35), Sheriff Brady stops to speak with Mrs. Mills. From across the street, Pastor Taylor Ealy sees Brady laugh. It's April Fool's Day.

After his light-hearted exchange with Mrs. Mills, Sheriff Brady hurries to catch up with his men.

When the lawmen pass John Tunstall's store, a storm of bullets sweep the street. Shooting from behind a 10-foot-high adobe wall, the concealed gunmen mow down Brady and Deputy Hindman. The sheriff has been hit by a dozen bullets.

Sitting in the middle of the road, Sheriff Brady groans, "Oh, Lord," as he tries to rise, but another volley of shots riddles his body. He falls over, dead.

Deputy Hindman moans and cries out for water. Ike Stockton emerges from his saloon, rushes up the street and attempts to pull the wounded deputy to safety. As he does, Hindman is hit again. He dies in the street.

The shooting stops. It is quiet except for the distant barking of dogs.

Suddenly, two men sprint from the Tunstall corral into the street. "Big Jim" French covers William Bonney (a.k.a. Billy Kid). The Kid straddles Brady's body, perhaps looking for warrants or wanting to retrieve the Winchester rifle

Billy Kid stands on a wooden crate as he peers over the adobe wall. He must have a borrowed rifle, for Sheriff William Brady has taken his.

the sheriff took from him on February 20 (see sidebar on p. 34).

From his position in the Cisneros' front yard, Deputy Mathews takes aim and fires. His bullet clips Billy Kid's hip and rips through French's left thigh.

The Kid gives up his scavenger hunt, and he and French hotfoot it back to the safety of the corral.

Tunstall's main pard Rob Widenmann opens the north gate of the corral and all the Regulators mount their horses except French, who can't swing his leg over the saddle.

Six horses thunder out of the compound, heading east along the Bonito River bottom, unseen by the deputies up on the main road. As the Regulators meet the road just east of the Ellis Store, however, they are fired upon by the deputies. But the boys are out of range, and they escape.

Pastor Ealy quickly dresses French's thigh. ("I drew a silk handkerchief through the wound," Ealy later says.)

Comrades of the dead sheriff soon come looking for the perpetrators, but French is successfully hidden under the floorboards of Tunstall's store. He later escapes.

★

Sheriff William Brady (on horseback) exchanges greetings with a local as he rides in from his ranch, east of Lincoln. Across the street (behind Brady) is the Patron store. The Montaño store is farther up the street (same side) and houses Ike Stockton's saloon. Curling smoke, from the early morning cook fires, adds to the tattered, low hanging clouds left over from a rain storm that drenched the village. Not long afterwards, Brady and his deputies are ambushed as they walk past the Tunstall store (below).

Behind the corral wall are: Frank MacNab, "Big Jim" French, Fred Waite, U.S. Deputy Marshal Rob Widenmann (feeding the dogs, lower right), John Middleton, Henry Brown and Billy Kid.

Billy vs Brady Back Story

Sheriff William Brady arrested Billy Kid and two others on February 20, 1878, when the Kid tried to serve the sheriff and his deputies with warrants for the murder of John Tunstall.

The two warring factions in the Lincoln County War: Murphy-Dolan vs. McSween-Tunstall had been fighting over the mercantile and ranching interests in Lincoln County. As things turned nasty, Tunstall was murdered by a rogue element of Sheriff Brady's posse. Subsequently, the Kid and Richard Brewer swore affidavits against the posse members, including Brady, and got murder warrants issued by a friendly judge in a nearby town.

But instead of surrendering, Sheriff Brady and his deputies overpowered Billy and two fellow Regulators. Adding insult to injury, Brady took the Kid's Winchester (allegedly given to Billy by Tunstall).

The Kid was further humiliated when Brady imprisoned him in Lincoln's notorious pit jail. To boot, while he was in the hole, Billy missed Tunstall's funeral.

So Billy Kid had plenty of motives for the ambush. Plus, he wanted to retrieve his favorite weapon.

The night before the ambush, the Kid and other Regulators slipped into Lincoln, unnoticed, and ensconced themselves in the Tunstall store and corral. Technically part of Rob Widenmann's posse, the crew was determined to gain control of Tunstall's property. Sheriff Brady had previously commandeered the estate until Widenmann and soldiers from Fort Stanton forcibly evicted Brady's men.

Debate still rages over whether the Regulators planned this ambush, or if they merely saw an opportune moment. Also debated is the purpose behind Brady and his deputies' walk down Lincoln's main street. Some historians say Brady was going to the courthouse to post an official affidavit, while others claim he and his deputies were planning to arrest lawyer Alexander McSween when he rode into town.

Logic would dictate you don't need four armed deputies to post an affidavit. It's probably safe to say, the lawmen were going to arrest McSween, and in fact, he did arrive shortly after the ambush and rode by the dead sheriff who was still lying in the street.

Just east of John Tunstall's store, Sheriff William Brady and Deputy George Hindman (left) are hit on the first volley fired by the Regulators (above). Most of the Regulators probably participate in the shooting (Widenmann will claim he was feeding the dogs at the time), but only one of them will be sentenced to hang for the killings.

"We heard shooting and looked up to see William Brady fall to a sitting position. He said, 'Oh Lord' and tried to get up, but there was just another round of shots and he fell back mortally wounded."

—*Gorgonio Wilson*
eyewitness to the gunfight

Sheriff Brady, holding Billy Kid's Winchester.

In John Tunstall's Corral

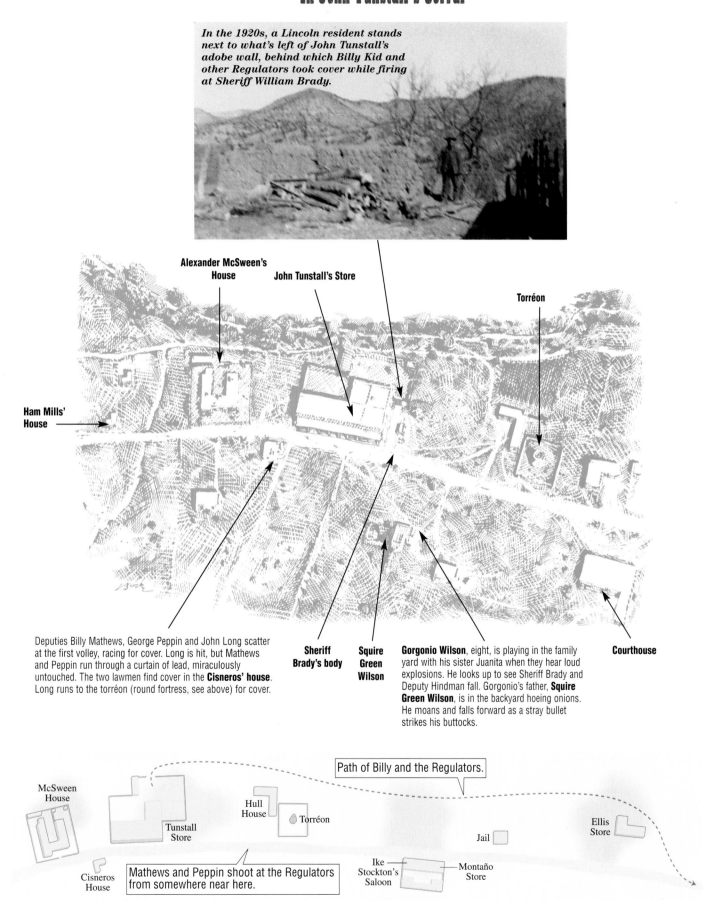

In the 1920s, a Lincoln resident stands next to what's left of John Tunstall's adobe wall, behind which Billy Kid and other Regulators took cover while firing at Sheriff William Brady.

Alexander McSween's House

John Tunstall's Store

Torréon

Ham Mills' House

Deputies Billy Mathews, George Peppin and John Long scatter at the first volley, racing for cover. Long is hit, but Mathews and Peppin run through a curtain of lead, miraculously untouched. The two lawmen find cover in the **Cisneros' house**. Long runs to the torréon (round fortress, see above) for cover.

Sheriff Brady's body

Squire Green Wilson

Gorgonio Wilson, eight, is playing in the family yard with his sister Juanita when they hear loud explosions. He looks up to see Sheriff Brady and Deputy Hindman fall. Gorgonio's father, **Squire Green Wilson**, is in the backyard hoeing onions. He moans and falls forward as a stray bullet strikes his buttocks.

Courthouse

McSween House

Tunstall Store

Hull House

Torréon

Path of Billy and the Regulators.

Jail

Ellis Store

Cisneros House

Mathews and Peppin shoot at the Regulators from somewhere near here.

Ike Stockton's Saloon

Montaño Store

Sheriff William Brady (above) and Jimmie Dolan (right).

Jacob "Billy" Mathews

The House

Taken after the name of Dolan's store, "the House" was the term for supporters of the Murphy-Dolan side.

Sheriff William Brady (above, at left) was a Murphy-Dolan man who saw Alexander McSween and John Tunstall as interlopers, carpetbaggers and worse (most of the Dolan men were Roman Catholic while McSween and Tunstall were Protestant). Jimmie Dolan (above, at right) was a hotheaded Irishman who was every bit as deadly as Billy Kid. Jacob "Billy" Mathews (left) survived the ambush and lived until June 3, 1904.

Sheriff Brady and Deputy George Hindman were buried on the Brady property east of Lincoln (below).

Sheriff William Brady and Deputy George Hindman's graves on Brady's property, east of Lincoln, New Mexico. Hindman's headstone was later stolen and has never been replaced.

—Courtesy Carrell Collection, Lincoln County Heritage Trust —

Aftermath: Odds & Ends

The ambush and killing of Sheriff William Brady hurt the Regulators' credibility as a lawful entity and lost them sympathy for their cause.

— ☆ —

Three days after the Brady ambush, the Regulators landed at Blazer's Mill and shot it out with Buckshot Roberts (featured in *Classic Gunfights Vol. I*).

— ☆ —

Some three years later, Billy Kid (by then known as Billy the Kid) was captured and tried for killing Sheriff Brady. Found guilty and sentenced to hang, the Kid told a reporter, "I think it hard that I'm the only one to suffer the full consequence of the law." He had a point. Some seven men had shot at the sheriff, and it is unknown which of them killed the sheriff and his deputy. Although some lawyers believe the murder charge probably wouldn't hold up in court today, any betting man would agree that the best odds are with the House, and that it's safe to assume Billy was one of the killers.

— ☆ —

Recommended: *The Illustrated Life & Times of Billy the Kid* by Bob Boze Bell, published by Tri Star–Boze Publications; and *The Lincoln County War* by Frederick Nolan, published by University of Oklahoma Press.

Hidden under the floorboards of John Tunstall's store, "Big Jim" French later escapes and joins up with his friends.

Did Hollywood Ever Get it Right?

There have been 40-plus movies about Billy the Kid, but the closest account of Sheriff William Brady's murder appears in the 20th Century Fox/Morgan Creek Production, *Young Guns* (1988).

Open on a dusty street, as circus-like music plays.

[Sheriff William Brady and three deputies walk up the main street of Lincoln. Close-up on two Regulators peering through the wooden slats in a gate. They are watching Billy as he approaches the sheriff.]

First Regulator: "What the hell's he doin'?"

Second Regulator: "He ain't all there, is he?" Beat. "Is he?"

[As he gets closer to the sheriff, Billy Kid mimics the sheriff's walk (above). Finally, Billy Kid takes off his derby and throws it over Brady's head. The hat falls in the street directly in front of Brady, startling the sheriff. The Kid grabs both of Brady's pistols from his holsters and steps back. A surprised Brady turns in horror at his predicament.]

Billy: (gleefully) "Top of the mornin' to ya, girls."

[Billy shoots the sheriff point-blank. Brady reels back as the ball opens.

Everyone starts shooting. Chavez (*Lou Diamond Phillips*) rides in on horseback from around a corner and throws a knife, hitting one of the deputies in the neck. Doc Scurlock shoots from the top of a building, taking down one of the deputies trying to flee on horseback. The two Regulators, who were hiding behind the fence, run into the street and empty their pistols. When they realize they are out of bullets, the two scramble back inside the corral.

As the smoke clears, Billy steps up to a dying Brady and puts his foot on the sheriff's Winchester. Billy cocks his gun and aims it at the sheriff.]

Billy: "Reap the whirlwind, Sheriff Brady. Reap it!" (right)

[The blast of his gun turns into the flash of a photographer's exposure, as the famous Billy pose appears in high relief. Cut to a print of the photo. (In the movie, it's a nice looking 5 x 7 black and white print, but in reality, it was a small tintype.)

A lack of filming continuity is also apparent. When Billy shows his picture to his friend Alexander McSween, Billy's thumb is by his head in the photo. When he drops his arm, though, he is holding the photo where his feet are shown.

Billy Kid hands the photograph to McSween.]

Billy: "It's for you, Alex."

Alexander McSween: "You weren't supposed to touch Brady."

Billy: "Sheriff Brady sent the men who killed John. It was a good move for us, Alex."

McSween: (heatedly) "Was it Billy?"

Billy: (defensively) "Yes it was!"

[The other Regulators stand around, looking sheepish.]

McSween: "Have you seen the *Independence*?" [McSween pulls a clipping out of his coat pocket and hands it to Billy Kid.] "The governor has revoked your deputization powers. You're now wanted by the legitimate law as well as those outside the law. You're not only being hunted by John Kinney and Murphy's men, you're being hunted by troops. Fort Stanton, Billy, the U.S. Army. The governor's put a $200 bounty on your head."

[McSween starts walking away, but then he stops and turns back.]

"Reap the Whirlwind, Sheriff Brady. Reap it!"
—Billy Kid

McSween: "You were supposed to serve 11 warrants and expose the ring [the Santa Fe Ring—a group of special interest-minded businessmen]. Instead, you went out and you went on the warpath. On a rampage! Now Richard's [Dick Brewer] dead. We're living up here like fugitives. What the hell do you think you're doin' out there?"

Billy: "I don't know. Maybe I'm tryin' to get some attention."

Report Card

Four deputies, not three, walk with Brady, and all of the Regulators were hidden behind the high adobe wall at Tunstall's store. The swaggering street walk of the Kid is a screenwriter *(John Fusco)* invention and a bit of wishful thinking. **History: C-**

In spite of the historical improv, the spirit of the Kid's reckless daring is captured perfectly and McSween's diatribe at the Kid afterwards is no doubt close to what Alex probably said to his errant knights. **Movie Moment: A+**

Young Guns is available on DVD from Lions Gate.

HIGH DOOM IN THE ANDES

⸺ ☆ ⸺

BUTCH AND SUNDANCE VS AN UYUNI POSSE

⸺ ☆ ⸺

TWO MULES FOR ARAMAYO

⸺ ☆ ⸺

Butch and Sundance, high in the Andes.

NOVEMBER 6, 1908

Two heavily armed "Americanos, on jaded mules" ride into the high mountain village of San Vicente, Bolivia. As the sun is setting, Butch and Sundance rein in at the home of Bonifacio Casasola. A village official, Cleto Bellot, approaches the strangers and asks what they want.

"An inn," they tell him.

Bellot informs the strangers there are no inns in San Vicente, but that Casasola can put them up and sell them fodder for their mules.

After tending to their animals and unloading their gear, Butch and Sundance join Bellot in their room, which opens onto Casasola's walled patio. The Americans ask Bellot about the road to Santa Catalina, an Argentine town just south of the border (this was probably a ruse to throw off any pursuing posses) and the road to Uyuni (their real path), located about 75 miles north of San Vicente. They also ask where they can get sardines and beer, and Bellot sends Casasola to buy some with money provided by Sundance.

After more small talk, Bellot leaves and goes to the home of Manuel Barran, where a four-man posse from Uyuni is staying. The posse rode in that afternoon, warning Bellot and other locals to be on the lookout for two Yankees with a mule belonging to the Aramayo mining company, whose payroll was recently robbed.

The posse consists of Capt. Justo P. Concha, two soldiers from the Abaroa Regiment and Inspector Timoteo Rios from the Uyuni police department. Captain Concha is unavailable when Bellot arrives. When Bellot tells his news to Inspector Rios and the two soldiers, they immediately load their rifles.

Accompanied by Bellot, the three posse members march to Casasola's home and enter the patio. As the Bolivians approach the bandits' room, Butch appears in the doorway, draws his Colt and fires, hitting lead soldier Victor Torres in the neck. Torres gets off a shot with his rifle, then runs out the patio door and collapses at a nearby house. He dies within minutes.

The other soldier and Inspector Rios also return fire, before they scurry out with Bellot. After retrieving more ammunition, the two return and fire into the house through the patio door.

By now, it's dark. Captain Concha runs up and commands Bellot to find some locals who can watch the roof and the back of the adobe house so the bandits don't punch a hole and escape. As Bellot rushes to comply, he hears "three screams of desperation" coming from the bandits' room.

The San Vicenteños are finally at their posts, but the firing has ceased and all is quiet. Minutes turn into hours, and there's no response from the fugitives. The guards remain at their stations throughout the bitterly cold and windy night.

The next morning, Bellot and others enter the room and see Butch's lifeless form stretched out on the floor, one bullet wound in the temple and another in the arm. Sundance's corpse sits on a bench behind the door, hugging a large ceramic jar. He has been shot once in the forehead and several times in the arm. According to one report, the bullet removed from Sundance's forehead came from Butch's Colt. From the positions of the bodies and the locations of the fatal wounds, the witnesses conclude that Butch put his partner out of his misery, then turned his gun on himself.

☆

The Last Supper: Sardines & Beer.

BUTCH AND SUNDANCE'S LAST DAYS

Oruro 200 miles →

■ Uyuni

Quechisla

Río Atocha

Chorolque ▲ Mountain

■ **Atocha**

BOLIVIA

Probable route of the Uyuni posse.

Río Mochara

Peró's intended route.

Huaca Huañusca (Dead Cow Hill)
— BY ANNE MEADOWS —

Huaca Huañusca (Dead Cow Hill) ▲

November 4
After robbing Peró, Butch and Sundance retreat into a ravine.

November 4
Rounding Huaca Huañusca (Dead Cow Hill), they meet two armed men who demand the payroll.

Río Salo

San Vicente

Salo

November 6
Butch and Sundance arrive in San Vicente at sundown, unaware a four-man posse from Uyuni is also there.

Río Tatasi

Río Tupiza

Río Callco

November 3, 1908
Carlos Peró and party, carrying the Aramayo Company payroll, leave Tupiza for Quechisla, the center of the Aramayo mining operation.

Butch and Sundance's escape route.

Tupiza

Scale: Approximately 1:2,000,000 meters

Río Cucho

Cucho

November 6
About 10 miles beyond Estarca, the pair ask for directions to San Vicente.

Tomahuaico

November 4
Butch and Sundance spend the night at Tomahuaico.

Río San Juan

Estarca

Did You Know?
Bolivia is slightly smaller than Alaska or about three times the size of Montana. In 1908, the population was 2.3 million; and the size of the country was larger than it is today.

PERU   BRAZIL
Lake Titicaca
4 **BOLIVIA** 2
3 6
5 **San Vicente**
CHILE   PARAGUAY
7
Pacific Ocean
Buenos Aries ★   URUGUAY
Villa Mercedes
ARGENTINA
ANDES MTNS
Cholila   Atlantic Ocean
Ryan and Place ranch
Falkland Islands

1 Antofagasta: U.S. Vice-Counsel Frank Aller bailed Sundance out of some trouble with the Chilean government in late 1905. In 1909, Aller sought to establish Butch and Sundance's deaths in order to settle the latter's estate.

2 Concordia: Butch and Sundance worked at the Concordia tin mine in the central Bolivian Andes southeast of La Paz, from late 1906 to mid-1908.

3 Eucaliptus: A railroad construction camp payroll was held up twice in 1908— in April and August. Butch and Sundance were suspected of the holdups, but the evidence is scant.

4 La Paz: Butch and Sundance periodically visited Bolivia's capital, La Paz, during their work at Concordia, probably lodging at the Grand Hotel Guibert, where they first met the Concordia mine assistant, Percy Seibert.

5 Oruro: Sundance's last known mailing address was in Oruro, a city of 22,000, some 5,000 of whom were foreigners, chiefly connected with regional mining interests. Oruro may have been Butch and Sundance's intended destination after the Aramayo holdup.

6 Santa Cruz: Butch (and possibly Sundance) traveled to the city of Santa Cruz in the eastern Bolivian lowlands in November 1907 to explore buying a cattle ranch.

7 Tupiza: Looking for a bank to rob, Butch and Sundance took up residence here in Aug. 1908. The arrival of an army detachment in early November caused them to switch their plans to a mine company payroll outside of town.

From a c. 1910 postcard of the route to Estarca, part of Butch and Sundance's escape route.
— COURTESY DANIEL BUCK AND ANNE MEADOWS —

Butch and Sundance probably view this scenery while traveling the Tupiza-San Vicente road. The cactus at left are alborecentes or dawnbreakers.
— BY ANNE MEADOWS —

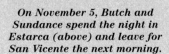

On November 5, Butch and Sundance spend the night in Estarca (above) and leave for San Vicente the next morning.
— COURTESY DORA SALAZAR—

Their Last Paycheck

At 9:30 a.m. on November 3, in Huaca Huañusca (Dead Cow Hill), Butch and Sundance confront a trio delivering the payroll from a local mining company, Aramayo Francke & Company. They demand the 80,000 *bolivianos* in the payroll. Manager Carlos Peró informs them that they are only carrying 15,000 *bolivianos* (worth about $6,000 in 1908); the larger payroll was not due for delivery until next week.

The unhappy bandits take the packet of bills, as well as one of the mules (perhaps to compensate for the missing loot), and retreat into a ravine. Peró alerts authorities once he reaches the village of Guadalupe. Military officers and miners, whose pay had been stolen, were soon combing the ravine and watching out for strangers in southern Bolivia.

The outlaws planned their escape well, though. By midnight, they reach Tomahuaico, the camp of British engineer, A.G. Francis, who they befriended during the year. Although Francis disapproves of their banditry, he allows them to spend the night. When news reaches them the following morning that the military is heading that way, Francis escorts the duo along the Río San Juan del Oro to the village of Estarca.

The next morning, they say goodbye to their friend and head on to Cucho, 10 miles north of Estarca. From there, they follow the trail into the Andes until reaching San Vicente—the end of the trail for them.

Goertz binoculars

Gray, narrow, soft-brimmed, felt hats

Gaiters (see ad below)

JAMES SMART

Carlos Peró.
– COURTESY FLORENCIA PERÓ URQUIDI –

"The two Yankees wore new, dark-red thin-wale corduroy suits with narrow, soft-brimmed hats, the brims turned down in such a way that, with the bandannas tied behind their ears, only their eyes could be seen. One of the bandits, the one who came closest to and talked with me, is thin and of normal stature, and the other, who always maintained a certain distance, is heavyset and taller. Both of them carried new carbines, which appeared to be of the Mauser-type . . . but they were completely new . . . The bandits also carried Colt revolvers, and I believe they also had very small Browning revolvers outside their cartridge belts, which were filled with rifle ammunition."

—*CARLOS PERÓ, DESCRIBING THE AMERICANOS WHO ROBBED HIM*

Both Butch and Sundance wore gaiters instead of boots during the robbery. At left is an ad for Polainas, *the Spanish word for the popular leggings.*
– COURTESY DANIEL BUCK AND ANNE MEADOWS –

Note the "Q" brand on Butch's mule, marking it as the property of the Aramayo mines.

Last known photograph of Butch and Sundance (above) in the Bolivian Andes, c. 1907. Butch is astride his mule and Sundance is tending his. Notice they are wearing the same style outfits from the Cholila ranch photo (p. 43) taken four years earlier. During the Aramayo holdup, Peró said the bandits were carrying "Goertz trihedral binoculars" (opposite page). In the inventory taken after the outlaws' deaths, there was only one saddle (an English saddle at that). Perhaps Butch used a makeshift saddle, or maybe someone purloined his saddle before the inventory.

INVENTORY OF MONEY AND PERSONAL EFFECTS FOUND ON THEIR BODIES AND IN THEIR BAGGAGE

ON BUTCH:

- One leather purse containing a paper on which the address of a La Paz post office box was written
- One six-shot Colt revolver with holster, belt and 30 cartridges
- One silver pocket watch with silver chain
- Two notebooks with several notations
- 16 pounds sterling
- Two half-pound sterling notes
- One silver coin worth five cents
- One unusable pocket mirror
- Two removable buttons
- One metal comb
- Seven cards inscribed Enrique B. Hutcheon
- Seven cards inscribed Edward Graydon
- One linen handkerchief
- One black pencil

IN THEIR BAGGAGE:

- Two saddle blankets
- One cotton blanket
- One Bolivian poncho
- One plain English saddle
- One pair of iron spurs
- One triangular file (in the saddlebags)
- One pair of leather saddlebags
- Two unusable silk handkerchiefs
- One pair of chamois gloves
- One pair of wool socks
- One used towel
- One map of Bolivia
- 88 pounds sterling
- 14,400 *bolivianos* (Aramayo payroll)
- Cartridges for Colt revolvers and Mauser & Winchester carbines
- One used bridle
- One saddle skin
- One cinch
- One Mauser carbine and scabbard
- One pair of binoculars
- Three cotton handkerchiefs
- One saddle blanket
- One set of reins
- One whip

ON SUNDANCE:

- One 18-karat gold watch, number 93,220, without crystal
- One leather and metal lasso
- Bills and coins of various denominations from Bolivian banks, totaling 93 *bolivianos* and five cents
- One nickel penknife
- One English dictionary
- Two linen handkerchiefs
- One ordinary pocket mirror
- Nine removable shirt buttons
- Two cuff links
- Eight small wooden or bone buttons
- One waterproof cloak
- 121 Winchester cartridges
- One new modified Winchester carbine

July 1923 bird's-eye view of San Vicente sheeted in snow, looking northeast (probably from the local silver mine). Arrows mark the death house (lower right) and the cemetery where the outlaws' bodies were buried. They came in on one of the roads at right.

– BY VICTOR J. HAMPTON / COURTESY MARIQUITA HOLLIDAY –

What were they thinking when they topped the rise at 14,500 feet and started their final descent into Hell?

In the Midst of Society

After viewing this 1901 copy of the portrait of the Sundance Kid and Ethel, taken before they left Manhattan for Argentina, William Pinkerton wrote in a letter to his brother Robert what "a great pity we did not get the information regarding this photograph while this party was in New York. It shows how daring these men are, and while you are looking for them in the wilderness and mountains they are in the midst of society."

Sundance and Ethel certainly had hid well in society. The lovers rang in the 19th century by spending New Year's Eve in New Orleans. Then they traveled to Pennsylvania, where Ethel met her beau's brother and sisters. After that, they enjoyed Turkish baths in Buffalo, New York, and saw the majestic Niagara Falls.

They reunited with Butch in New York City on February 1, checking in at a boarding house as a Wyoming cattle buyer, his wife and her brother. During their tour of the city, this famous photo of Ethel and Sundance was taken at the De Young Studio. On February 20, they were off, steaming away on the British ship *Herminius*, heading to Argentina to build a new life.

The crimes committed by the Wild Bunch were recorded by U.S. authorities as an aid in capturing the elusive duo. Their files included Butch Cassidy's prisoner record from Wyoming (below left) and the Sundance Kid's police file, which would later be translated (below right) and posted in South America where the duo was hiding out.

FORM 55-3-101-10M-AE.

P. N. D. A. .... No.

NAME......George Parker.   No. 469 R

ALIAS......"Butch" Cassidy; George Cassidy; Ingerfield.

NATIVITY....United States.   COLOR......White

OCCUPATION...........:......Cowboy; rustler

CRIMINAL OCCUPATION ....Bank robber, highwayman, cattle and horse thief

AGE......37 yrs (1902).   HEIGHT.....5 ft. 9 in

WEIGHT....165 lbs....   BUILD...... Medium

COMPLEXION .... Light

COLOR OF HAIR.........................Flaxen

EYES...........Blue.   NOSE......................

STYLE OF BEARD .....Mustache; sandy, if any

REMARKS:—Two cut scars back of head, small scar under left eye, small brown mole calf of leg. "Butch" Cassidy is known as a criminal principally in Wyoming, Utah, Idaho, Colorado and Nevada and has served time in Wyoming State penitentiary at Laramie for grand larceny, but was pardoned January 19th, 1896. Wanted for robbery First National Bank, Winnemucca, Nevada, September 19th, 1900 See Information No. 421.

..OS RETRATOS, SEÑAS PERSONALES Y LA HISTORIA CRIMINAL DE CADA UNO DE LOS INDIVIDUOS SOSPECHOSOS, SE DAN Á CONTINUACIÓN.

NOMBRE......Harry Longbaugh, (a) "Kid" Longbaugh, (a) Harry Alonzo, (a) Frank Jones, (a) Frank Boly, (a) el "Sundance Kid."

NACIONALIDAD......sueco-americano......PROFESION..........Vaquero; tratante

OCUPACIÓN CRIMINAL......Salteador de caminos, ladrón de bancos, de ganado y de caballos.

EDAD......35 años.....................ESTATURA......5 pies 10 pulgadas

PESO......de 165 á 175 libras.....................CONSTITUCION......Buena

OJOS......Azules ó pardos.....................COLOR......Trigueño claro

BIGOTE Ó BARBA......[si tiene] castaño natural con matiz rojizo.

FACCIONES......tipo griego.....................NARIZ......Más bien larga

COLOR DEL PELO......castaño, puede habérselo teñido; se peina pompadour.

ES ESTEVADO Y TIENE LOS PIES MUY SEPARADOS.

OBSERVACIONES ......Harry Longbaugh estuvo 18 meses cumpliendo sentencia en la cárcel de Sundance, Condado de Cook, Wyoming, cuandoera muchacho, por robo de caballos.   En Diciembre de 1892, Harry Longbaugh, Bill Madden y Henry Bass asaltaron un tren del Ferrocarril "Great Northern" en Malta, Montana.   Bass y Madden fueron juzgados por este crimen y sentenciados á 10 y 14 años de presidio, respectivamente; Longbaugh se escapó y desde entonces es un prófugo.   En 28 de Junio de 1897 y bajo el nombre de Frank Jones, Longbaugh en compañía de Harry Logan (a) Curry, Tom Day y Walter Putney, tomó parte en el robo de un banco en Belle Fourche, South Dakota.   Todos cayeron en manos de la policía, pero Longbaugh y Harvey Logan lograron escaparse de la cárcel de Deadwood, en 31 de Octubre del mismo año.   Desde entonces Longbaugh no ha vuelto á estar preso.

HARRY LONGBAUGH.
Retrato tomado el 21 de Noviembre de 1900.

This photo shows the Sundance Kid, Ethel Place and Butch Cassidy getting ready to have tea on their Cholila ranch in 1903. The photo was sent to a family member and remained in the family for many years until it was published in 1992.

– COPYRIGHTED BY PAUL D. ERNST –

Ranching in Cholila

James "Santiago" Ryan, Harry "Enrique" A. Place and Ethel Place deposited $12,000 in gold notes (worth about $240,000 today) at the Banco de Londres y Río de la Plata after arriving in Buenos Aires in February 1901.

They traveled south to Chubut, settling on the Cholila Valley, finding land along the eastern shore of the Río Blanco that was perfect for a ranch. Once the log ranch buildings were constructed, they bought 16 colts for 855 pesos (about $7,500 today). In October, they registered three brands (see below).

"I like the place better everyday. I have 300 cattle, 1500 sheep, and 28 good Saddle horses, 2 men to do my work, also a good 4-room house, wearhouse [sic], stable, chicken house and some chickens … the country is first class," Butch wrote in an August 10, 1902, letter to Mrs. Davies, the mother-in-law of his outlaw pal, Elzy Lay.

Unfortunately, they had to abandon their ranch in 1905 when local police began suspecting the Yankees of robberies in the area.

Soon after arriving in Cholila, Butch and Sundance registered three brands: (from top to bottom) Sundance (Place), Butch and Sundance (Ryan and Place) and Butch (Ryan).

– FROM THE GUIA DE LA PATAGONIA / COURTESY DANIEL BUCK AND ANNE MEADOWS –

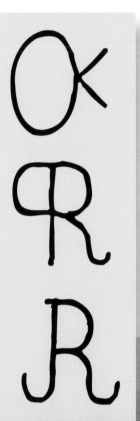

Butch (far left), Sundance and Ethel (far right) and six neighbors in front of the trio's cabin in Cholila, c. 1904. Butch and Sundance are sporting Montana Peak hats, and the saddles are Western style.

– COURTESY JONES FAMILY –

The Wild Bunch's Hole-in-the-Wall hideout in Wyoming was so remote and untamed, it attracted Presidential Sportsman Theodore Roosevelt, as noted by this account in the March 15, 1903, issue of The New York World.

– COURTESY DANIEL BUCK AND ANNE MEADOWS –

Tupiza policeman making an arrest (left). A Bolivian miner (right) shows off his hardware. These are the types of brave Bolivians Butch & Sundance run into in San Vicente.

– Courtesy Daniel Buck and Anne Meadows –

As the three Uyuni posse members approach the Casasola home, Butch Cassidy suddenly appears in the doorway and begins firing.

Patio of house, c.1922, where Butch and Sundance die.

– By Victor J. Hampton –

The bodies of Butch Cassidy and the Sundance Kid were buried in the local cemetery that afternoon. The Aramayo payroll was found intact in their saddlebags. Once the outlaws' possessions had been inventoried (see p. 41), Capt. Justo P. Concha absconded to Uyuni with the lot, leaving the Aramayo company to battle for months in court to recover its money and mule.

Two weeks after the shoot-out, the bandits' bodies were disinterred, and Carlos Peró (the Aramayo manager) identified them as the same pair who had held him up. Tupiza officials conducted an inquest of the robbery and shoot-out, interviewing Peró, Bellot and several others, but were unable to ascertain the dead outlaws' names.

In July 1909, Frank D. Aller, the American vice-consul in Chile who had known Sundance, wrote the American legation in La Paz, requesting the death certificates for Frank Boyd or H.A. Brown and Maxwell, who were reportedly "killed at San Vicente near Tupiza by natives and police and buried as desconocidos." Boyd had been Sundance's alias in Chile; Brown and Maxwell were aliases that he and Butch had used in Northern Bolivia. Aller needed the certificates to settle Boyd's estate in Chile. The legation forwarded his request to the Bolivian foreign ministry, stating that the Americans had "held up several of the Bolivian Railway Company's pay trains, as also the stage coaches of several mines, and . . . were killed in a fight with soldiers that were detached to capture them as outlaws."

Numerous stories circulated about Butch cheating death in Bolivia and returning to the States. (Sometimes Sundance is included, but most legends name only Butch.) The most persistent tale is that put forth by Lula Parker Betenson, one of Butch's sisters, who insisted that Butch had visited the family in 1925. Others in the family disagree, saying that Butch never returned, but Lula still has her believers.

In 1937, an elderly Matt Warner, a former member of the Wild Bunch, scribbled a note to historian Charles Kelly: "Forget all the reports on Butch Cassidy, they are fake. There is no such man living as Butch Cassidy. His real name was Robert Parker, born and raised in Circle Valley, Utah and killed in South America, he and a man by the name of Longwow [sic] we[re] killed in a soldier post their [sic] in a gun fight. This is straight."

Recommended: *Diggging Up Butch & Sundance* by Anne Meadows, published by University of Nebraska Press; *Sundance, My Uncle* by Donna Ernst, published by The Early West.

KILL BILL!

Just who is the mystery man with the shotgun in the cane break?

— ☆ —

BILL DOOLIN
vs
THE DUNN BROTHERS & HECK THOMAS

— ☆ —

OUTLAW "CLEVERLY RIDDLED" WITH BUCKSHOT

— ☆ —

Bill Doolin gets it!

AUGUST 25, 1896

Riding with a six-man posse that includes the deadly Dunn brothers, U.S. Marshal Heck Thomas meets two informants (the Noble brothers, Tom and Charles) outside of the crossroads settlement Lawson, Oklahoma. The rendezvous has been prearranged for sundown, just beyond the village.

With the informants in tow, the posse makes its way to the west end of the tiny berg. The men are after Bill Doolin, who has been on the run since his spectacular break from the Guthrie federal jail on July 5.

Moving stealthily, the posse takes position in a cane break straddling both sides of a dirt road leading west from the crossroads (see overview, opposite page). Meanwhile, Marshal Thomas crawls up on a hilltop and scouts the village with field glasses.

At the posse's approach, the Ellsworths' dogs begin barking. Since the Noble brothers have a blacksmith shop near the Ellsworth store, Doolin tells his wife "That must be those God damned Nobles. I'm going out and run them off."

Leaving Edith by the loaded wagon, Doolin walks his horse west along the country lane leading from the Ellsworth barn. In the moonlit darkness, he carries his Winchester and peers into the foliage on both sides of the road. When Doolin approaches the cane break at the bottom of a small hill, Thomas cries out "Halt!" A voice from the other side of the road yells, "Stop! Throw up your hands!"

Doolin shoulders his Winchester and fires toward the voices. He then drops his rifle (evidence suggests it was shot out of his hands) and snaps off several quick shots with his revolver.

A volley of Winchesters firing from both sides of the road replies, followed by the boom of a double-barreled shotgun. Doolin is riddled with buckshot and "razed" to the ground.

The fight is over.

The Heck Thomas Version

"We waited a long time without seeing anyone, although there was considerable stir about the store and dugout. We learned afterwards that Doolin's wife had told him some of the neighborhood boys had been spying around there too much and that someone was around that night. Finally [Doolin] came out of the stable and to our great surprise, started down the lane coming west, you know how the store is situated on the high prairie.... If Bill had wanted to have made his escape he could have had open roads north, south, east, northeast, or ... northwest through the pasture to those high hills that you have seen many times. Well, he came right down the lane leading his horse by the tip ends of the bridle reins, walking slow in the bright moonlight, Winchester in both hands, well out in front of him, nearly in position to shoot. He was sure on the prowl ... looking first to one side and then the other ... for the neighborhood boys who had been spying on him. Then I hollowed to him and had one of the other boys on the other side of the road to hollow to him.... He shot at me and the bullet passed between me and B. Dunn. I had let one of the boys have my Winchester and had an old No. 8 shotgun. It was too long in the breech and I couldn't handle it quick so he got another shot with his Winchester and as he dropped his Winchester from [a] glancing shot, he jerked his pistol and some of the boys thought he shot once and the others twice—and about that time I got the shotgun to work and the fight was over."

—Heck Thomas, in a letter to Bill Tilghman, September 3, 1896

A Spectacular Jail Break

On Sunday, July 5, 1896, at 8:45 p.m., a prisoner in the "bull pen" of the Guthrie federal jail asked a guard to move a bucket of water closer to the cells. When night guard J.T. Tull leaned over to move the bucket, prisoner George Lane reached through the bars and grabbed the guard, holding him as three others disarmed him and got the keys. Once out of his cell, Bill Doolin (above) grabbed another guard's pistol from a box and, along with eight others, made his escape into the darkness. For the rest of his movements, see map at right.

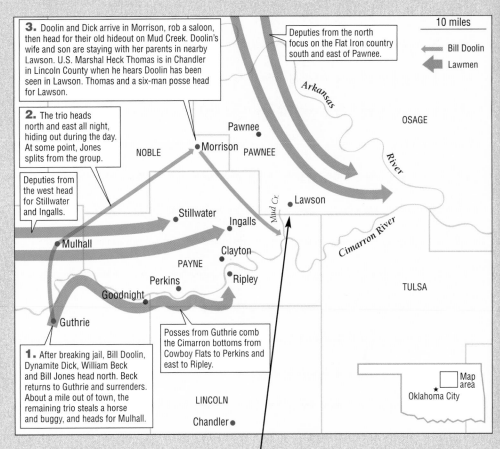

3. Doolin and Dick arrive in Morrison, rob a saloon, then head for their old hideout on Mud Creek. Doolin's wife and son are staying with her parents in nearby Lawson. U.S. Marshal Heck Thomas is in Chandler in Lincoln County when he hears Doolin has been seen in Lawson. Thomas and a six-man posse head for Lawson.

2. The trio heads north and east all night, hiding out during the day. At some point, Jones splits from the group.

Deputies from the west head for Stillwater and Ingalls.

Deputies from the north focus on the Flat Iron country south and east of Pawnee.

← Bill Doolin
← Lawmen

10 miles

OSAGE

Arkansas

River

Pawnee

NOBLE

Morrison

PAWNEE

Mud Cr.

Lawson

Stillwater

Ingalls

Cimarron River

Mulhall

Clayton

PAYNE

TULSA

Perkins

Ripley

Goodnight

1. After breaking jail, Bill Doolin, Dynamite Dick, William Beck and Bill Jones head north. Beck returns to Guthrie and surrenders. About a mile out of town, the remaining trio steals a horse and buggy, and heads for Mulhall.

Guthrie

Posses from Guthrie comb the Cimarron bottoms from Cowboy Flats to Perkins and east to Ripley.

LINCOLN

Chandler

Map area

Oklahoma City

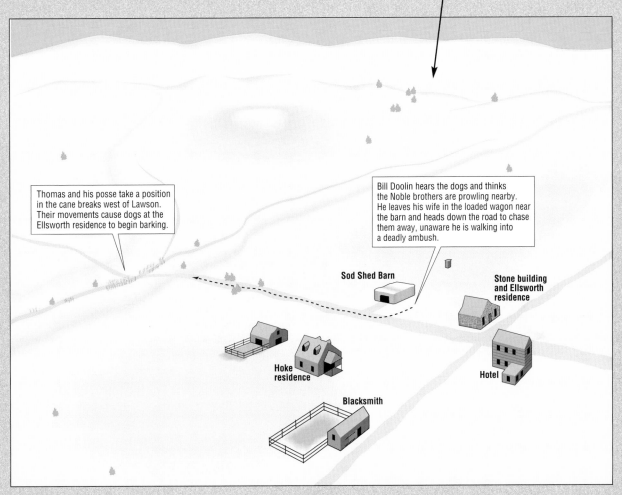

Thomas and his posse take a position in the cane breaks west of Lawson. Their movements cause dogs at the Ellsworth residence to begin barking.

Bill Doolin hears the dogs and thinks the Noble brothers are prowling nearby. He leaves his wife in the loaded wagon near the barn and heads down the road to chase them away, unaware he is walking into a deadly ambush.

Sod Shed Barn

Stone building and Ellsworth residence

Hoke residence

Hotel

Blacksmith

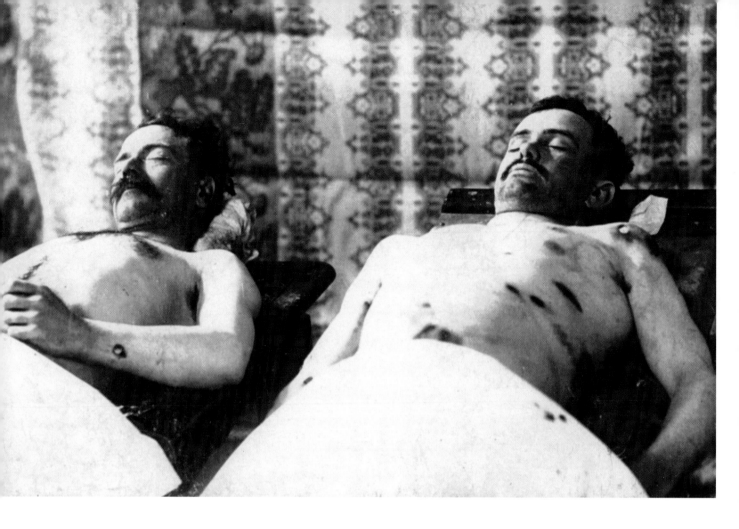

A Dark and Persistent Rumor Stalks the Dunn Brothers

After the killing, a wagon was procured from the Hoke farm (see map, p. 47) and the dead body of Doolin was carted back to Guthrie to be photographed for the reward (see photo, p. 50). Because Doolin's corpse had an absence of bloodstains when it was delivered to the morgue, rumors claimed the outlaw had died a natural death, was set up against a tree (one version says a "corn shock") and filled with buckshot in order to "make believe he had been killed." Another version claimed Doolin died of "galloping consumption" and was then shot. Actually, Doolin had "bled profusely" and was cleaned up for the photo at W.B. Dougherty's photography studio.

The dark rumors undoubtedly gained credence because the Dunn brothers (right) were notorious for playing both sides of the law. Having ridden with the Daltons and Doolin on the Owlhoot Trail, they abruptly switched sides. A year prior to the Doolin shooting, they had killed two other fellow gang members, George "Bitter Creek" Newcomb and Charley Pierce, while they were guests in the Dunn home. Killed for the

John and Dal (above), just two of the deadly Dunn brothers, who not only waylaid Bill Doolin, but who also ambushed George "Bitter Creek" Newcomb and Charley Pierce (top), seen here in a grisly morgue shot.

– DUNN BROTHERS PHOTO TRUE WEST ARCHIVES –

reward, the dead outlaws had buckshot in the heels of their feet, leading many to infer they were shot as they slept.

In the aftermath of the Doolin shooting, members of the Thomas posse were reluctant to say who had used the shotgun. Some historians maintain that one of the

Dunns fired the fatal shotgun blast that brought down Doolin, adding that Thomas only claimed to be the shooter because it would be easier to collect the reward.

Mrs. Edith Doolin

Outlaw Bill Doolin fell in love with a Methodist minister's daughter who was working at the O.K. Hotel in the outlaw stronghold of Ingalls, Oklahoma. After courting for several months, Bill and Edith Ellsworth (left) eloped to Kingfisher, Kansas, and on March 15, 1893, they married.

Born in Marshalltown, Iowa, in 1873, Edith was one of 13 children, only nine of whom survived to adulthood. At five feet six inches tall, Edith Doolin weighed a little over 100 pounds, had dark, penetrating eyes and "moved with a decisive step—with the air of one who knew what she was about." She stood by her outlaw husband, defending and protecting him to the end.

In a running gun battle after the train robbery in Cimarron on June 10, 1893, lawman Chris Madsen (above, at left) fired a Winchester .30-30 and clipped Doolin in the right heel, the ball coursing over the arch and shattering the bone in the ball of his foot. This wound never properly healed, and Doolin developed a painful "rheumatic condition." Three years later, in January 1896, Bill Tilghman (above, at right) arrested Doolin, who was seeking relief at a Eureka Springs, Arkansas, resort.

Heck Thomas

A lawman from the age of 18, Henry Andrew "Heck" Thomas (at left) wore a U.S. marshal's badge at the time of the Doolin slaying. Known as the "three guardsmen," Thomas, Chris Madsen and Bill Tilghman helped clean out most of the Doolin-Dalton Gang. Thomas was wounded a half dozen times during his storied career. He died of Bright's disease on August 15, 1912.

The identity of the woman in the photo is unknown, but collector Robert G. McCubbin believes it may be either Lottie or Florence Hitchcock, sisters who worked as clerks in the U.S. Marshal's office in Guthrie.

H. T. Swearingen,
PHOTOGRAPHER.

Opposite Post Office,
GUTHRIE, O. T.

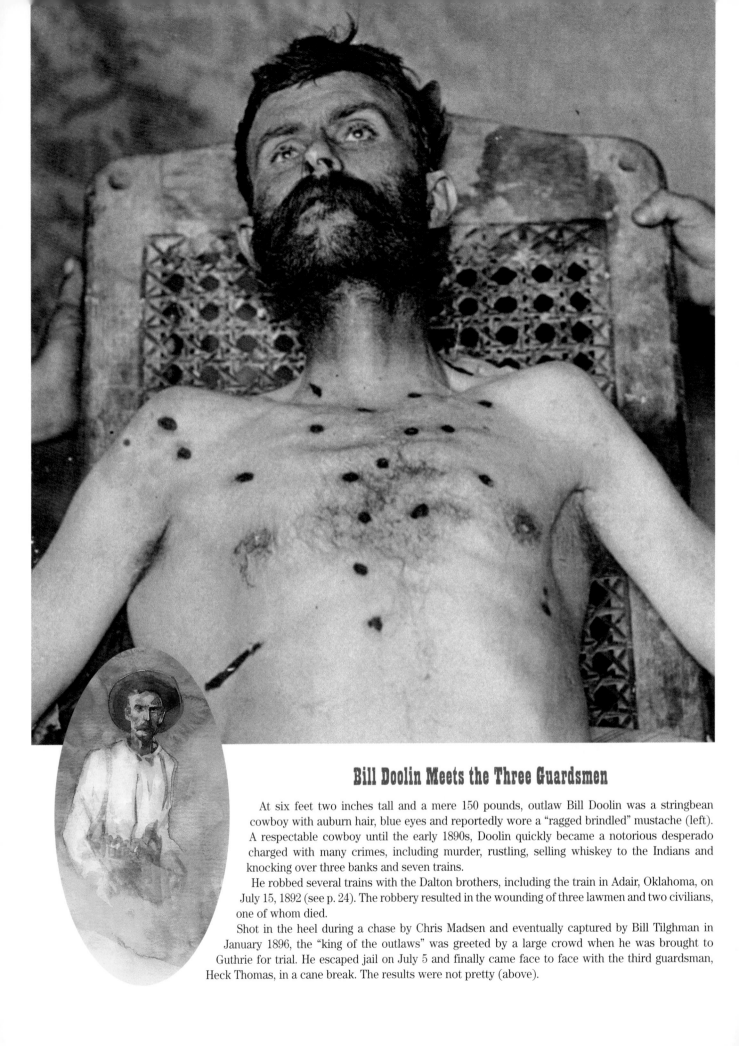

Bill Doolin Meets the Three Guardsmen

At six feet two inches tall and a mere 150 pounds, outlaw Bill Doolin was a stringbean cowboy with auburn hair, blue eyes and reportedly wore a "ragged brindled" mustache (left). A respectable cowboy until the early 1890s, Doolin quickly became a notorious desperado charged with many crimes, including murder, rustling, selling whiskey to the Indians and knocking over three banks and seven trains.

He robbed several trains with the Dalton brothers, including the train in Adair, Oklahoma, on July 15, 1892 (see p. 24). The robbery resulted in the wounding of three lawmen and two civilians, one of whom died.

Shot in the heel during a chase by Chris Madsen and eventually captured by Bill Tilghman in January 1896, the "king of the outlaws" was greeted by a large crowd when he was brought to Guthrie for trial. He escaped jail on July 5 and finally came face to face with the third guardsman, Heck Thomas, in a cane break. The results were not pretty (above).

> "Two features of Doolin's make up were his dark, glassy, penetrating eyes, his thin lips and canine teeth. Doolin suffered intensely from rheumatism and his celebrated left leg was rendered almost useless by that ailment."
>
> —*Guthrie Leader*

Bill Doolin flashes a stolen silver dollar.

Subscription Forwarded to Hell

Returning from a successful train robbery with the Daltons, Bill Doolin met a newspaperman on the trail. After asking about lawdogs on the back trail, Doolin rode on but then turned and asked how much a subscription to the paper cost. Informed a one-year subscription was a dollar, Doolin reached into a "shot sack," scooped out a handful of stolen silver dollars and threw them at the journalist. Dismounting and picking them up, the scribe informed Doolin they would pay for 11 years and then asked him where he should send the paper. The outlaw laughed and told him to send the paper to Ingalls until he was dead, and thereafter, to hell.

Aftermath: Odds & Ends

In spite of posted rewards for Bill Doolin that reached $5,000, when it came time to pay up, Heck Thomas received only $1,425, which he split among the posse members. After paying a lawyer to write up the "applications for reward" and two stenographers, and the expense of a half-dozen trips to Kansas, Missouri and Arkansas in order to facilitate the collection of the above reward money, lawman Thomas was "out of pocket," meaning he had spent more money than he received.

Only two mourners were present when Bill Doolin was buried on August 29: his wife Edith and a family friend. A twisted, rusty buggy axle was thrust into the ground for a grave marker. Edith filed a $50,000 damage suit for the "unlawful death" of her husband but later withdrew it.

Edith soon remarried, and Doolin's son Jay took the name of his stepfather (Meek). Jay lived in Ponca City, Oklahoma, and worked for an oil company before retiring at age 65. He once wrote, "I have never been arrested for a crime, nor has any one of my children. This is not true of some of the Oklahoma Territory marshals. Although Bill Doolin was never praised for his law enforcement, he never had an outlaw son." Jay was coyly referring to lawman Bill Tilghman's nefarious sons (two were lifelong criminals and a third died from gunshot wounds while trying to hold up a crap game).

Recommended: *West of Hell's Fringe* by Glenn Shirley, published by University of Oklahoma Press; and *Bill Doolin: Outlaw O.T.* by Colonel Bailey C. Hanes, published by University of Oklahoma Press.

"I SHOULD HAVE KILLED THEM ALL"

JESSE EVANS
GANG
VS
TEXAS RANGERS

One Ranger falls while trying to load another shell into his Winchester.

JULY 2-3, 1880

Outlaw Jesse Evans and three of his gang saddle up and head for the Mexican border. In Fort Davis, Texas, they have been tipped off to the arrest of their compadre, Capt. John Tyson (real name John Selman).

Stopping in Presidio, Texas, just shy of the Mexican border (see map, opposite page), Evans openly buys a new pair of boots in an apparent attempt to convince authorities that he is on the way out of the country. Instead, Evans and crew make a feint towards Old Mexico, then head northwest towards a hideout in the Chinati Mountains.

Riding all night and covering some 70 miles, a Texas Ranger patrol led by Sgt. Ed Sieker stops to water its horses on Cibola Creek, 18 miles north of Presidio. One of the Rangers notices a group of riders up on a distant ridge watching them. Using field glasses, the Rangers take a closer look, and as they do, the men on the mountainside move away.

Riding forward to investigate, the Rangers soon take fire as the four horsemen mount up and head to the higher ridges. A running gunfight ensues for over a mile as the outlaws climb higher and higher up the range.

Trapped at the ridgeline, the four outlaws dismount and make a stand behind a rock outcropping. Led by Sgt. Sieker, the Rangers also dismount and charge forward, firing. Ranger D.T. Carson gets outlaw George Graham in the side, but Graham keeps firing down at the advancing lawmen. As Graham peeks up for another shot, Sgt. Sieker shoots the outlaw in the head, killing him instantly.

Seeing Graham fall, the outlaws raise their hands and surrender. The Rangers quickly run up to the fortified position and disarm their prisoners.

Only after the surrender do the Rangers realize that one of their squad has been killed. While looking for a knife lost during the fight, Ranger L.B. Caruthers discovers the body of Ranger George Bingham, lying behind a bush, his lifeless hands gripping his Winchester. From his position on the ground, the Rangers theorize that he was gamely trying to pump another round in the magazine at the time of death.

Sieker later states, "I should have killed them all."

Fire on the Mountain: The Texas Rangers advance aggressively, pouring lead into the outlaws' position. Four horses are killed in the fusillade.

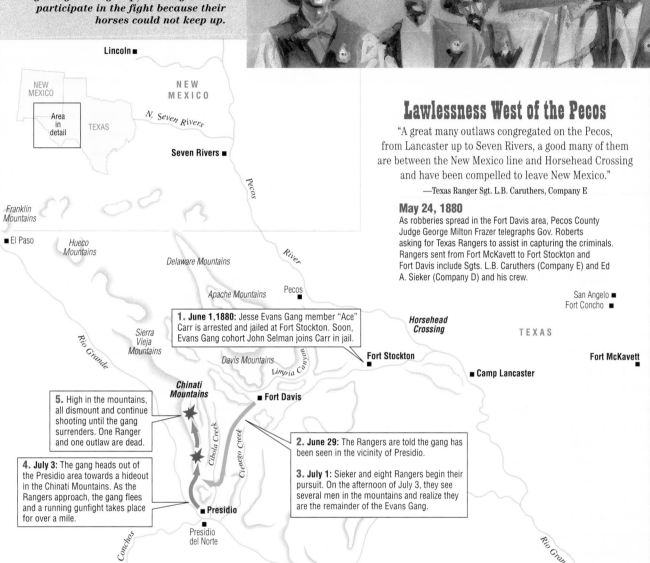

Lawlessness West of the Pecos

"A great many outlaws congregated on the Pecos, from Lancaster up to Seven Rivers, a good many of them are between the New Mexico line and Horsehead Crossing and have been compelled to leave New Mexico."

—Texas Ranger Sgt. L.B. Caruthers, Company E

May 24, 1880

As robberies spread in the Fort Davis area, Pecos County Judge George Milton Frazer telegraphs Gov. Roberts asking for Texas Rangers to assist in capturing the criminals. Rangers sent from Fort McKavett to Fort Stockton and Fort Davis include Sgts. L.B. Caruthers (Company E) and Ed A. Sieker (Company D) and his crew.

1. June 1, 1880: Jesse Evans Gang member "Ace" Carr is arrested and jailed at Fort Stockton. Soon, Evans Gang cohort John Selman joins Carr in jail.

5. High in the mountains, all dismount and continue shooting until the gang surrenders. One Ranger and one outlaw are dead.

4. July 3: The gang heads out of the Presidio area towards a hideout in the Chinati Mountains. As the Rangers approach, the gang flees and a running gunfight takes place for over a mile.

2. June 29: The Rangers are told the gang has been seen in the vicinity of Presidio.

3. July 1: Sieker and eight Rangers begin their pursuit. On the afternoon of July 3, they see several men in the mountains and realize they are the remainder of the Evans Gang.

20 miles

Fort Davis, 1886.

Established in 1853, Fort Davis saw much action during the expedition against Mescalero Apaches. Abandoned at the start of the Civil War, Fort Davis passed back and forth between the Union and Confederacy until it was sacked by Mescaleros in 1862. The Army returned in 1867 and in 1880, the fort's soldiers were involved in the Victorio War. Its troops left for good in 1891, and for a while, the abandoned buildings served as summer retreats for West Texans. In 1963, Fort Davis became a part of the National Park Service.

The Bat Cave Jail—so-called because the jail cell was one large hole with no light—in Fort Davis, Texas. While incarcerated here, Jesse Evans wrote to Billy the Kid (left) asking Billy to come to his rescue. He refers to Billy as Antrum, for Antrim, which was the Kid's stepfather's name.

– JAIL PHOTO COURTESY PHILIP J. RASCH COLLECTION / OLD LINCOLN COUNTY MEMORIAL COMMISSION –

Billy the Kid and Jesse Evans

The Kid is believed to have first met Evans in the fall of 1877 soon after Billy killed his first man near Camp Grant, Arizona, and fled back to the Silver City, New Mexico, area. Riding with Jesse and other members of a loose-knit gang of rustlers known as "The Boys," Billy and Jesse caroused in the Mesilla-El Paso area. Legend says that the Kid eventually gravitated to Lincoln County via Seven Rivers, while Jesse and the Boys went up the Tularosa side of the mountain.

Ironically, the two landed on opposite sides of the fence in the brewing Lincoln County War, with Jesse riding for the House (Dolan and Murphy) and the Kid riding for Tunstall (and McSween). Both bravos survived the war and each other.

On the night of February 18, 1879, they decided to make peace. Stepping out from hiding on either side of Lincoln's only street, the two shook hands and vowed to formally end hostilities.

The truce lasted only several hours as the celebrating, drunken entourage stumbled across Susan McSween's lawyer on the street. Two of Jesse's buddies, Billy Campbell and probably also Jimmie Dolan, started taunting the lawyer with their guns, which went off, killing the lawyer. The group then sauntered over to another saloon, but upon second thought, someone asked the Kid to place a pistol on the body to make it seem as if the lawyer had been armed. The Kid did the task and skinned out for Fort Sumner. That's the last time the two outlaws saw each other.

So it's more than a little ironic that when Jesse Evans landed in the pit jail in Fort Davis, Texas, he wrote a letter to the Kid (of all people), asking him to come save him. The letter suggests a stronger bond than most would have expected.

So why didn't the Kid help out Jesse? The answer is found in Ranger C.L. Nevill's report of August 26, 1880:

"The prisoners are getting restless. I have a letter they wrote to a friend of Evans in New Mexico calling himself Billy Antrum to

Texas Rangers, Company D, Frontier Battalion, 1885.

– COURTESY TEXAS RANGER HALL OF FAME AND MUSEUM –

cause their rescue, and to use the words he was 'in a damned tight place only 14 Rangers here any time, ten on scout and only four in camp now,' and that Antrum and a few men could take them out very easy and if he could not do it now to meet him [Evans] on the road to Huntsville [prison] as he was certain to go. I understand this man Antrum is a fugitive from somewhere and a noted desperado. If he comes down and I expect he will, I will enlist him for a while and put him in the same mess with Evans & Co."

The authorities intercepted that letter, and even though the Ranger suspected another would get out to Billy, no record of such exists. It is likely Jesse had no idea his letter was intercepted, and when the Kid didn't come, he made other plans.

Billy the Kid (center, at left) warily shakes hands with his Lincoln County foe and former riding pard Jesse Evans. After the handshake, the assembled group retired to a saloon and wrote up a formal contract of peace, which lasted but a few hours.

It was through the Chinati Mountain range, some of which is shown above, that members of the Texas Ranger Frontier Battalion chased the Evans Gang.

– COURTESY CHUCK PARSONS –

The Bad Guys:

- Jesse Evans. Went by a host of aliases. Captured.
- Charles Graham, alias Charles Gross, Graves, Groves. Captured.
- August Gross, alias Gunter. Captured.
- George Graham. Probably went by alias of Gross, Graves, Davis, Evans, etc. Killed.
- John Selman, alias Gunter, Gross, Captain Tyson. In Jail.
- Albert Graham, alias "Ace" Carr. In Jail.

The body of Ranger Bingham is found while Ranger Caruthers is looking for his knife.

A Dashing, But Short Outlaw

Jesse Evans: Born in 1853, five feet, three-quarters inches tall, weighing 150 pounds, with fair complexion, gray eyes and light hair. He has two large scars on the left thigh, one above his left elbow and another below.

Aftermath: Odds & Ends

John Selman was sent to Texas' Shackelford County, where they evidently didn't want him much because they put him on a nag and told him to "ride hard, fast, and far," as the authorities fired their pistols in the air for added inducement. Selman landed in El Paso, Texas, where he took up the badge and later became notorious for killing John Wesley Hardin.

⟨☆⟩

Jesse Evans was found guilty of second-degree murder and sentenced to 10 years in the state prison at Huntsville Penitentiary. Arriving at Huntsville on December 1, 1880, Evans entered as prisoner #9078. Almost 18 months later, on May 23, 1882, Evans went over the wall and disappeared from history.

⟨☆⟩

The Graham brothers hired a better lawyer (thanks to a wealthy father) and skipped out on the charges after being released on bond.

⟨☆⟩

August Gross joined Jesse at the Huntsville Penitentiary. He was reportedly released after three or four years and returned to Fort Davis to live out his days.

⟨☆⟩

Recommended: *Jessie Evans: Lincoln County Badman* by Grady E. McCright & James H. Powell, published by Creative Publishing Company.

CHALK LEVEL SHOOT-OUT

⁕

THE YOUNGERS VS THE PINKERTONS

⁕

SHOT DOWN IN THE MISSOURI WILDS

⁕

BLOODY DUEL ON HORSEBACK

⁕

John Younger (left) looks quite innocent, while his older brother Jim (in a disputed photo) looks the part of an outlaw.

– TRUE WEST ARCHIVES –

MARCH 17, 1874

round 2:10 p.m., the Snuffer family and John and Jim Younger are sitting down for dinner at Theodrick Snuffer's homestead.

As they eat, the Youngers hear horses coming up the lane so they quickly scramble up a ladder into the attic. Peering through a crack between the logs, they see two strangers telling old man Snuffer they're "cattle buyers." One of the riders asks Snuffer for directions to Widow Simms' (or Sims') house, as she advertised livestock for sale. Snuffer points the way, but the two ride off in the wrong direction.

John becomes suspicious and wants to follow them. Jim demurs, stressing he isn't looking for trouble, and he sits down to finish his meal. John presses his argument, pointing out that both strangers are too well armed to be simple cattle buyers and that the younger of the two looked nervous.

Jim finally gives in and agrees to accompany his younger brother. The two gather their horses from the Snuffer shed and give chase.

Three-quarters of a mile up the road, the two "cattle buyers," Louis Lull and Ed Daniels, join up with James Wright, who is from the area and stayed behind because he was afraid the Snuffers would recognize him. The trio converse about their search for the James-Younger Gang while riding their horses at a slow gait.

When the Youngers approach on horseback, Wright pulls his pistol, spurs his horse and gallops away, cutting across a field as fast as his horse can carry him (ironically, heading east toward Widow Simms' house). Jim orders Wright to stop, and when he doesn't, Jim fires a pistol ball that takes off Wright's hat.

John has both barrels of his double-barreled shotgun cocked. He covers Lull and Daniels until Jim rejoins them. The Youngers order the two strangers to give up their guns. Both men comply, dropping their revolvers on the road. Jim dismounts to gather the weapons, which include Lull's English-made .43 caliber Tranter, a Pinkerton standard issue.

Holding up the exotic pistol for his brother to see, Jim says, "John, these are damn fine guns. It's sure nice of these boys to make us a present of them." Jim then turns back to the prisoners and asks, "Where you fellas from?"

"We're from Osceola," Lull replies.

"What are you doin' out here?"

"Just ramblin' around."

John cuts in, "You sure you're not detectives looking for someone?" He tells them detectives have been up here hunting them all the time, and they are going to stop it.

> "John, these are damn fine guns. It's sure nice of these boys to make us a present of them."
>
> —*Jim Younger*

"I am no detective," Daniels says. "I can show you who I am and where I belong."

One of the Youngers admits to having met Daniels in town, so he turns to Lull and demands: "What the hell are you riding around here with all them pistols on for?"

"Good God," Lull pleads. "Is not every man wearing them that is traveling and have I not as much right to wear them as anyone else?"

"Hold on, young man," John barks. "We don't want any of that."

John lowers his shotgun for a moment. (One report says John was trying to "quiet his horse.") With John's attention diverted, Lull reaches behind and pulls out a small No. 2 Smith & Wesson pistol and fires. Lull's horse lurches forward just as the bullet strikes John's neck. Reacting, John pulls the trigger on his shotgun and the pellets hit Lull in the shoulder and arm.

Lull barely manages to stay in the saddle as his horse explodes down

Continued on p. 58

Lull's Tranter pistol was manufactured in Birmingham, England, and exported to the South during the Civil War. The Pinkerton detective agency later bought a surplus of these firearms and issued them to men in the field. The Tranter was a .36 caliber (or .38), six-shot double action with a 4½-inch barrel.

Lull gives up two pistols when he drops them in the roadway. The other pistol make is unknown. Lull's hideout pistol is a .32 caliber rimfire Model No. 2 Smith & Wesson, which needed to be cocked before firing. Lull amazingly pulls it from concealment and cocks, aims and fires it before John Younger can react.

Both Jim Younger (above, left) and John are heavily armed as they ride to confront the suspicious men. After the gunfight, an eyewitness reports, "I think James Younger took four revolvers off of John Younger," in addition to John's shotgun.

The Younger family home on 100 acres of prime farmland in **Lee's Summit, Jackson County**. In 1862, the Youngers had five different farms in Jackson and Cass Counties.

– COURTESY JACKSON COUNTY HISTORICAL SOCIETY –

Kearney, Clay County
Location of the Jesse James farm.

Harrisonville, Cass County
Location of Henry Younger's livery stable and dry goods store.

– COURTESY CASS COUNTY HISTORICAL SOCIETY –

H. W. YOUNGER
ON HAND ONCE MORE!

SPRING & SUMMER GOODS!

DRY GOODS
BOOTS, SHOES,
HATS & CAPS,

MISSOURI

St. Clair County
Location of the McFerrin Negro Settlement near Monegaw Springs. After the fight, the wounded Capt. Lull and the body of John Younger will be brought to the McFerrin cabin pictured at left.

Gad's Hill, Wayne County
Location of the Iron Mountain Railroad robbery. The Youngers are suspects in the theft.

Cole and John Younger, c. early 1870s.

The Younger Brothers

All four brothers—Cole, 30; Jim, 26; John, 23; and Bob, 21—are suspected of participating in several robberies, including the Gad's Hill train robbery. The boys travel in pairs and move around continuously. They spend little time in their home county (see map) but occasionally stop in St. Clair County, where they visit friends, such as the Snuffers. For the most part, they spend their nights in the McFerrin Negro Settlement, three miles southeast of Monegaw Springs, where they stay with John McFerrin and his wife Hannah, who worked for the Younger family in Jackson County. The McFerrin home is a safe haven until the Pinkertons begin to close in.

Continued from p. 56

the road. On horseback, Daniels attempts to follow suit, but Jim shoots him in the neck. Daniels falls off the back of his mount onto the roadway.

Down the road, Lull has no control over his horse as it jumps "into the bushes and the trees." Lull later says he tried to get ahold of the reins with his right hand to "bring him on the road," but John "rode by me and fired two shots at me, one of which took effect in my left side, and I lost control of my horse and he turned into the brush and a small tree struck me and knocked me out of the saddle."

Meanwhile, Jim rolls Daniels over and immediately sees his death stare. Jim looks up and sees John coming back from the grove. He calls out his brother's name. John quizzically stares at his older brother, then slowly falls sideways, landing on the other side of a fence.

Jim runs to John's side, but his brother is dead. Lull's bullet severed John's jugular vein. (It's amazing he lived as long as he did.)

Born in Boston, Massachusetts, Edwin B. Daniels is a part-time deputy from Osceola. For many years, this photograph has been published as being Daniels, even though the subject seems a bit old for a man of 23.

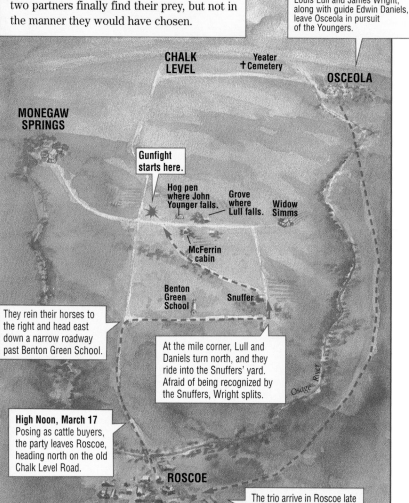

The Pinkerton Posse

Captain Lull has traveled all over Missouri—searching for the Youngers, riding with different posses, stopping at dozens of farms and dwellings, seeking information on the whereabouts of the Youngers. Lull and his two partners finally find their prey, but not in the manner they would have chosen.

March 16, 1874
Louis Lull and James Wright, along with guide Edwin Daniels, leave Osceola in pursuit of the Youngers.

CHALK LEVEL   Yeater † Cemetery   OSCEOLA

MONEGAW SPRINGS

Gunfight starts here.

Hog pen where John Younger falls.   Grove where Lull falls.   Widow Simms

McFerrin cabin

Benton Green School   Snuffer

They rein their horses to the right and head east down a narrow roadway past Benton Green School.

At the mile corner, Lull and Daniels turn north, and they ride into the Snuffers' yard. Afraid of being recognized by the Snuffers, Wright splits.

Osage River

High Noon, March 17
Posing as cattle buyers, the party leaves Roscoe, heading north on the old Chalk Level Road.

ROSCOE

The trio arrive in Roscoe late in the evening and put up for the night in the Roscoe Hotel.

Neck & Neck

The doctors who examined the dead men reported the bullet that killed John Younger "entered the right side of his neck, touching the clavical [sic] bone on the upper side, and about two inches from the meredian [sic], went nearly straight through the neck ... Edwin B. Daniels, came to his death from the effect of a gunshot wound, which entered the left side of the neck, about one inch from the meredian line, about midway of the neck, opposite the aesophagus [sic] ... went nearly straight through the neck, striking the bone; the orifice was pretty large, indicating that the ball was of a pretty large size." The report named Jim Younger as the killer of Daniels.

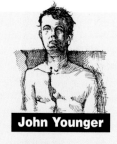

John Younger

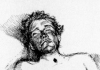

Ed Daniels

Why Did Captain Lull Resort to Deadly Force?

Severely wounded, Lull, still claiming he is W.J. Allen, gave the following statement to the coroner's inquest:

"[The Youngers] said detectives had been up there hunting for them all the time, and they were going to stop it. . . ." John Younger "then lowered the gun, cocked it in a threatening manner. . . . I concluded that they intended to kill us. I reached my hand behind me and drew a No. 2 Smith & Wesson pistol and cocked it and fired at the one on horseback, and my horse frightened at the report of the pistol and turned to run, I heard two shots and my left arm fell, and then I had no control over my horse. . . ."

At the time of the gunfight, Lull's mind may have been consumed with the fate of fellow undercover Pinkerton agent J.W. Wicher, who was found murdered near Kearney, Missouri, only seven days earlier, on March 10. It is rumored Jesse James and others got him.

Just three months prior to this road battle, the Youngers surprised a posse from Appleton City who had ridden to Monegaw Springs to capture the brothers. Taking the offensive, the Youngers captured the posse and confiscated their weapons. But after a stern warning, the Youngers released them.

Perhaps the Youngers intended to do the same with Lull and Daniels. We will never know.

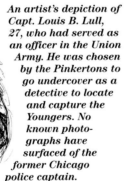

An artist's depiction of Capt. Louis B. Lull, 27, who had served as an officer in the Union Army. He was chosen by the Pinkertons to go undercover as a detective to locate and capture the Youngers. No known photographs have surfaced of the former Chicago police captain.

The cattle buyers' alibi seems especially shady when James Wright (a.k.a. John Boyle and Duckworth; age unknown) pulls his pistol and puts his spurs to his horse (left) as the Youngers approach.

Aftermath: Odds & Ends

Jim Younger removed his brother's pistols, watch and other personal effects. Mounting John's horse, Jim asked a neighbor who had witnessed the fight to take care of his brother's body. Then Jim rode up Chalk Road in the direction Detective James Wright had fled. Unable to find him, Jim returned to the Snuffer cabin to ensure John would be buried properly and then headed south to Arkansas to inform his brothers, Cole and Bob, about John's death.

* * *

Incredibly, Lull wasn't killed outright by the shotgun blast to his shoulder and arm, or the pistol shot to his chest. Found by a farmer, Lull was taken to a nearby cabin and, later that evening, was placed in a spring wagon and driven to Roscoe. A town doctor declared that the wounded detective would live, but, after several days, the Pinkertons reported Lull's condition had worsened and he died. Many in St. Clair County believed this to be a ruse and that the detective hadn't died, but that he just needed protection from the Youngers' wrath. In spite of this rumor, hundreds of Chicago policemen attended Lull's funeral and the former captain—or an empty casket—was laid to rest in a spacious Chicago cemetery.

* * *

After filing a report with Sheriff Johnson in Osceola, Detective Wright was never heard from again.

* * *

John Younger was first buried under a large cedar tree near the Snuffer cabin, where his shallow grave could be guarded. Later, his body was interred in the nearby Yeater Cemetery. The Snuffers and friends buried John at an angle, with his head pointed northwest, so they could later recognize the grave. (They were afraid to mark the grave lest the anti-Younger faction come to desecrate it.)

* * *

Two years later, Jim participated with his brothers, Cole and Bob, in the botched raid on a Northfield, Minnesota, bank (see *Classic Gunfights Vol. I*). Jim was badly wounded and captured in the Hanska Slough shoot-out two weeks later (as were Cole and Bob). He served 25 years in prison, was partially pardoned (with the restriction that he had to remain in Minnesota) and committed suicide in 1902.

Recommended: *The Outlaw Youngers: A Confederate Brotherhood* by Marley Brant, published by Madison Books; and "The Roscoe Gunfight" by Wilbur Zink.

THE TALE OF THE EMPTY CHAMBER

BILLY THE KID VS JOE GRANT

In December 1880, Billy the Kid will write a letter from Fort Sumner to Lew Wallace, the governor of New Mexico, claiming he, the Kid, isn't the "captain" of any gang.

"William Bonney" shows up on the 1880 census, living next door to Charlie Bowdre and his wife, Manuela, in the abandoned Indian Hospital at Old Fort Sumner (see map).

Bob Hargrove's saloon in Old Fort Sumner, New Mexico, is packed with cowboys, including James Chisum, brother of John, and three of his cowhands. Chisum and his men have been invited to take a drink with Billy the Kid, who enters the saloon with them.

Joe Grant, a newcomer to the area, notices the cowboys enter and snatches an ivory-handled pistol from Jack Finan's holster while, at the same time, putting his own pistol in the cowboy's holster.

The Kid steps up to him and says, "That's a beauty, Joe." The Kid takes the pistol from Grant's hand and spins the cylinder, checking at the same time to see how much ammunition it contains (three cartridges). He purposely moves the cylinder so that the next load will be a failure, then he returns the revolver to Grant.

"Pard," says Grant, as he sneers at the Kid, "I'll kill a man quicker'n you will for the whiskey."

"What do you want to kill anybody for?" asks the Kid, flashing his winning smile. "Put up your pistol and let's drink."

Grant moves behind the bar and starts viciously knocking about glasses and decanters with his pistol.

"Let me help you break up your housekeeping, Pard," says the Kid, drawing his own pistol and joining in the glass breaking.

Grant suddenly stops and eyes James Chisum. "I want to kill John Chisum, anyhow, the damned old—"

"You've got the wrong pig by the ear, Joe," says the Kid. "That's not John Chisum."

"That's a lie," shouts Grant. "I know better." And with that, he turns, points his pistol at the Kid and pulls the trigger. Instead of an explosion, the gun clicks loudly. Cussing, Grant raises the hammer for another shot, but before he can thumb it, a ball from the Kid's revolver crashes through his brains. He collapses behind the counter.

Emptying his spent shell, the Kid remarks, "Unfortunate fool; I've been there too often to let a fellow of your caliber overhaul my baggage. Wonder if he's a specimen of Texas desperadoes."

A bystander wonders aloud whether Grant has been killed and warns the Kid to watch out. Billy smiles and says, "No fear, the corpse is there, sure, ready for the undertaker."

Billy later dismisses the Joe Grant shooting as "a game of two, and I got there first."

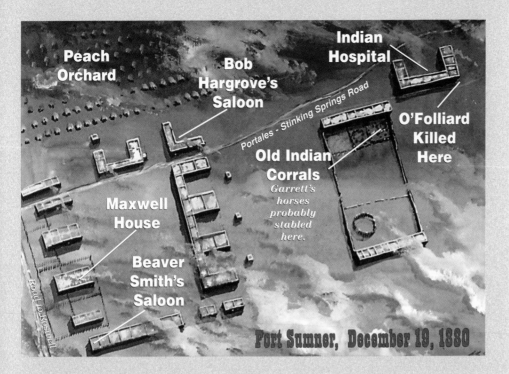

Peach Orchard

Bob Hargrove's Saloon

Indian Hospital

Portales - Stinking Springs Road

O'Folliard Killed Here

Old Indian Corrals
Garrett's horses probably stabled here.

Maxwell House

Beaver Smith's Saloon

Road to Roswell

Fort Sumner, December 19, 1880

On December 19, 1880, Sheriff-elect Pat Garrett and a posse of west Texas cowboys ambush Billy and his gang at the old Indian Hospital, then shoot and kill the Kid's neighbor, Charlie Bowdre (below), at Stinking Springs. The posse brings Billy and the rest of his gang back to Sumner, where Billy is allowed to kiss his sweetheart, Paulita Maxwell (left), before being transported by wagon to Las Vegas, New Mexico.

While being held at the jail in Las Vegas, the Kid is brought outside so the crowds can gawk at the captured celebrity. Perhaps as amazed as anyone, Billy later remarks to a reporter: "There was a big crowd gazing at me, wasn't there?"

Aftermath: Odds & Ends

Some scholars debate whether the Grant fight actually took place. Passed down by Jim Chisum's son, the details of the shooting became part of the folklore around Fort Sumner and the "facts" in the case are mighty slim. Still, the fight has the ring of truth to many Billy scholars and is generally accepted as being a bona fide event because the Chisums are a trustworthy source; also the newspaper quote from Billy (see bottom of p. 60) helps to substantiate the shooting.

— ☆ —

Billy the Kid continued rustling cattle (mostly Chisum's) in the Fort Sumner area and also demanded $500 from John Chisum for services rendered to the Tunstall-McSween cause during the late Lincoln County War. John declined to pay, and Billy vowed he would "steal from your cattle until I get it."

— ☆ —

A former Fort Sumner resident, Pat Garrett, was elected sheriff in November 1880. He was backed by John Chisum with specific orders to "clean out that squad east of Sumner." Garrett did just that, killing gang members "Chuck" Bowdre and Tom O'Folliard, and capturing the Kid at Stinking Springs, east of Sumner, and delivering him to the authorities in Santa Fe (see *Classic Gunfights Vol. I*).

— ☆ —

The Kid was tried for the killing of Sheriff Brady (see p. 32), convicted and sentenced to hang, but he escaped, killing his two guards. He made his way back to Fort Sumner where he was subsequently shot to death by Sheriff Pat Garrett in Pete Maxwell's bedroom on July 14, 1881.

— ☆ —

Recommended: Pat F. Garrett's *The Authentic Life of Billy the Kid* annotated by Frederick Nolan, published by the University of Oklahoma Press.

CHRISTMAS SPOILS

THE TIBURCIO VASQUEZ GANG VS KINGSTON, CALIFORNIA

OUTLAWS ATTEMPT TO ROB AN ENTIRE TOWN!

A dozen outlaws clatter across the Kingston bridge, their gun barrels glistening in the California moonlight.

Riding on a rumor of post-Christmas bounty, a Mexican gang headed by the notorious Tiburcio Vasquez reins up on the north bank of the Kings River, in northern California, and ties up their horses in a clump of willows.

In the evening darkness, 10 (some reports state 12) heavily armed raiders walk stealthily across the bridge with the goal of robbing the entire village of Kingston, nestled on the south side of the river. The town is small—two stores, a hotel, a blacksmith shop and several saloons.

The robbers encounter several citizens on the main street. They tie up each one and force them to lie face down in the street. Then the gang robs the citizens of their money and valuables. One of them, Milt Woods, refuses to lie down, protesting that doing so would spoil his good clothes. Incredibly, the outlaws give in and march him to the hotel so he can lie down there.

Having cleared the road, the bandits sweep across the open plaza. Vasquez carries four Colt Navy revolvers on his person as he strides boldly from store to store, commanding his men. As the premises are secured, Vasquez places a guard in front of each business.

Almost a dozen patrons are in the hotel saloon when the outlaws burst into the room with pistols at full cock. They force everyone to lie down on the floor as each victim's hands and feet are tied, and then they frisk for valuables. A puppy bounds in and runs from one victim to another, licking their faces. "The men were to claim later that this was the worst part of the whole affair," the *Fresno Weekly Expositor* later reports.

Not all the townsmen give in so easily. In the dining room of the hotel, Lance Gilroy is eating dinner when an outlaw enters, brandishing a pistol. Miss Reichert sees it, screams and runs out the back. Looking up, Gilroy assumes the intruder has insulted the lady, so he picks up a chair and floors the robber. Gilroy is wrestled to the ground and beaten with a revolver, leaving him badly hurt.

John Sutherland, a local, prominent rancher and landowner, is in the hotel when the robberies start. He grabs his Henry rifle and rounds up several other townsfolk. They take cover near the river and across the street from the stores.

In the dim light, Sutherland spots one of the outlaws (later identified as Ramon) standing guard in front of Sweet's Store. Sutherland opens fire. The robber staggers inside and exclaims in Spanish to his compadres, "I'm shot!" He is dangerously wounded.

"Vamos!" (Let's go!), Vasquez shouts to his men as they flee from the buildings, carrying their plunder. Sutherland's little posse opens a blistering barrage at the outlaws. Vasquez and his men, primarily armed with pistols, have a hard time determining the direction of the gunshots and wildly return the fire.

Sutherland and another townie press the attack, following the brigands across the bridge. As the bandits leap into their saddles, a ball strikes Vasquez's lieutenant, Clodoveo Chavez, in the leg above the knee. Francisco Gomez, Vasquez's cousin, is wounded in the neck.

After firing some 40 shots, Sutherland and his men have run out of ammunition. They watch helplessly as the outlaws gallop off into the blackness.

The fight is over. Repercussions will follow.

★

Outlaw leader Tiburcio Vasquez reportedly carries four Colt Navy revolvers on his person.

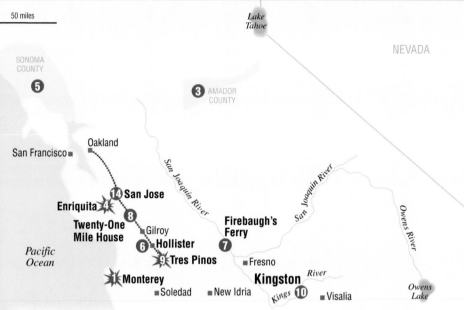

50 miles

Lake Tahoe

NEVADA

SONOMA COUNTY

5

Oakland

San Francisco

3 AMADOR COUNTY

San Joaquin River

San Joaquin River

Owens River

14 San Jose

Enriquita **4**

8

Twenty-One Mile House

Gilroy

Firebaugh's Ferry

Pacific Ocean

6 Hollister

7

9 Tres Pinos

Fresno

Monterey

Kingston

River

Soledad

New Idria

Kings **10**

Visalia

Owens Lake

Tulare Lake

Coyote Holes **11**

Panama

Bakersfield

2

LOS ANGELES COUNTY

12 **13**

Los Angeles

San Gabriel

Tiburcio Vasquez's Bloody Trail

1. 1854: Involved in the murder of a constable in Monterey.
2. 1857: Horse theft in Los Angeles County.
3. 1859: Escapes San Quentin; steals horses in Amador County; recaptured.
4. 1864: Stabs a butcher to death during a robbery in Enriquita.
5. 1866: Cattle rustling in Sonoma County.
6. 1871: Holds up stagecoach and travelers north of Hollister.
7. 1873: Leads a raid and robbery at Firebaugh's Ferry.
8. 1873: Raids and robs the Twenty-One Mile House between San Jose and Gilroy.
9. 1873: Vasquez and gang raid and rob Snyder's Store in Tres Pinos, killing three people.
10. 1873: Vasquez and gang sack the town of Kingston.
11. 1874: Robs the stage and teamsters at Coyote Holes Station.
12. 1874: Robs rancher and sheepman Alexander Repetto and three men in a wagon near Los Angeles.
13. 1874: Vasquez is captured at the house of Greek George on La Brea Rancho in what is now West Hollywood.
14. 1875: Vasquez is tried and hanged in San Jose.

Outrage and Exploitation

After the raid on Kingston, enraged "impromptu posses" scour the countryside, roughing up and threatening Mexicans up and down the coastal range. The governor of California, Newton Booth, is besieged with complaints about the roughshod treatment, and rumors are rampant. The *Fresno Weekly Expositor* accurately reports, "Rumor has hanged two Mexican thieves near Kingston."

A large reward is offered ($8,000 for Vasquez alive, $6,000 for him dead), and the governor commissions a party of manhunters, headed by Alameda County Sheriff Harry Morse, to run down the outlaws.

Vasquez is captured on May 13, 1874, near Los Angeles, by a posse led by Sheriff William Rowland. Vasquez becomes an instant celebrity. Various newspaper advertisements begin utilizing the bandit as an unpaid spokesman: "Vasquez says that Mendell Meyer has the Finest and Most Complete Stock of Dry Goods and Clothing." Female admirers send flowers, "exclusive" photos are sold on street corners and a play, "The Life of Vasquez," opens at the Merced Theatre. One report claims Sheriff Rowland turns down Vasquez's request to play himself.

A contemporary woodcut of Kingston, site of the Vasquez raid. The outlaws come across the bridge at lower right, commandeer the toll booth (just beyond bridge), then sweep across the plaza to the hotel, stores and saloons (center). The town posse led by John Sutherland hides itself in the brush along the banks in the foreground.

The real Tiburcio Vasquez (see at top and next page) dresses in conservative suits. Starting with the play, Vasquez's image becomes much more flamboyant (above).

The Two Tiburcios:

It's tempting to portray the bandido in high Spanish style (above), but he evidently dressed more like he is attired in the photo at right, even on raids. This photo was taken after his arrest in 1874.

The Tale of the Two Tiburcios

Legend has enhanced the image of Vasquez, so it's tempting to illustrate him with a high Spanish flair—a big sombrero, vaquero-style leggings, waist coat and concho-studded breeches and gunbelt. We can see him astride a strutting, black stallion, the outlaw's dark, black goatee glistening in the California moonlight, leading a large band of followers dressed just as dramatically, but not quite as dashing as El Jefe.

But when I asked my friend and author John Boessenecker if there are any contemporary descriptions of Tiburcio and the way he dressed, here's his reply:

"Sheriff Harry Morse obtained a description of Vasquez in early 1872 and wrote in his diary that Tiburcio wore a black coat trimmed with a beaver collar, black trousers and a black velvet vest decorated with floral designs from which protruded a silver watch chain and open-faced watch. By all accounts he always dressed like this—in fine and fashionable clothes, even while he was in the saddle and committing robberies."

"In appearance he is anything but the ferocious red-handed brigand his reputation has given him. He is a man of about medium stature, with a well-knit, wiry figure. He does not weigh over 140 or 150 pounds. His complexion is much lighter than the ordinary Mexican. His features are clear-cut, with an intelligent expression. His eyes are rather large and a light grey or blue in color. His forehead is high and his head well-shaped. In manner he is frank and earnest, with no disposition to make himself a hero. His general demeanor is that of a quiet, inoffensive man, and but for his calm, steady eye, which stamps him as a man of great determination and firmness, no one would take him for the terrible Tiburcio Vasquez."
—Los Angeles reporter, May 15, 1874

Tiburcio Vasquez.

Bradley & Bulofson. { Entered according to Act of Congress in the year 1874, by Bradley & Bulofson, } San Francisco.
in the office of the Librarian of Congress, at Washington

Awaiting the Hangman's Noose

Before his execution, Vasquez helps promote the earliest known "Crime Does Not Pay" campaign by signing various proclamations encouraging children to obey and listen to their parents, and certainly not to follow his example. When Tiburcio is shown the casket he is to be buried in, he reportedly remarks, "I can sleep here forever very well."

While awaiting his execution at a jail in San Jose, Vasquez has numerous visitors. On one day, he reportedly receives 673 visitors, 93 of them ladies.

On the day of his hanging, March 19, 1875, he stands on the gallows and turns toward Sheriff Adams. While the noose is tightened, he tells the sheriff, "Pronto!" meaning hurry up, let's get this over with. Tiburcio is buried in the old Santa Clara Mission Cemetery in Santa Clara, California.

Freedom Fighters or Gang Bangers?

The men who ride with Vasquez on the Kingston Raid are a rough group and they include his first lieutenant Clodoveo Chavez, Francisco Gomez, Blas Bicuna, Ramon Molina, Ysidro Padilla, Manuel Gomez, Ignacio Ranquel and one "Ramon" (no last name is known). The rest have never been positively identified. Most are hard cases and criminals. Padilla later leads his own gang and dies in prison. After a string of daring robberies, Chavez flees to Arizona, only to be gunned down by bounty hunters who cut off his head for identification so they can collect the $2,000 reward.

Vasquez Remembered Well

In California, Tiburcio Vasquez is not only remembered—in more than one place, the bandit is honored.

A high school and public park in southern California's Santa Clarita Valley are named after him. And the Tiburcio Vasquez Health Center provides services to the uninsured of Alameda County. Then there's the Vasquez Rocks, north of Los Angeles, where many Westerns have been filmed (see Roy Rogers' posse, above).

Not bad for a robber and convicted killer, who is seen today by many as an avenging hero, fighting for his country and his people.

Aftermath: Odds & Ends

The robbery of an entire town took less than a half hour and netted Tiburcio Vasquez's band more than $2,500 in money and jewelry, but they reportedly expected much more haul than they actually stole. Perhaps disheartened by their take, the bandits made a feint at the nearby town of Visalia, then split up and scattered.

⭐

The morning after the robbery, a three-man posse led by John Sutherland discovered a Mexican in some bushes about four miles outside Kingston. Initially, he confessed that he was one of the party. When he was jailed in Millerton, though, the suspect claimed he was robbed of $20 by the outlaws and forced to join them in their raid.

⭐

While Vasquez's men Clodoveo Chavez and Francisco Gomez recovered from their wounds, Ramon (last name unknown) was fatally wounded. His body was later found and exhumed at the notorious outlaw hideout called Rancho de los Californios, west of Fresno.

⭐

As the news of the robbery spread, other towns fielded posses, including Millerton, Visalia, Bakersfield, Tehachapi and Los Angeles. Vasquez had a large reward hanging on his head ($8,000 alive and $6,000 dead). He was captured while hiding out near Los Angeles. Tried and convicted for murder, the outlaw was hanged in San Jose on March 19, 1875.

⭐

Recommended: Bill Secrest, Sr.'s article on the Kingston raid in the *Quarterly of the National Association for Outlaw and Lawman History*, Vol. V. No. 1 (October 1979). Also look for John Boessenecker's forthcoming book on Vasquez, to be published in 2007.

LAWDOGS GO SOUTH

---✦---

HENRY NEWTON BROWN'S GANG VS MEDICINE LODGE COWBOYS

---✦---

A BAD DAY GETS WORSE. EVERYTHING THAT CAN GO WRONG, DOES.

---✦---

A heavy spring thundershower sweeps across Main Street in Medicine Lodge, Kansas, as four riders splash up Kansas Avenue from the west. They rein up to a coal shed behind the Medicine Valley Bank. While one man stays with the horses, three others walk briskly along the sidewalk. Two men enter the side door of the bank, while the third heads to the front door. The robber at the front door brandishes his Winchester and tells the two bankers to throw up their hands (perhaps because of the heavy rain, there are no customers in the bank). Cashier George Geppert complies, but bank President E.W. Payne, seated at his desk, reaches for a pistol.

Across the street from the bank, Reverend George Friedley hears gunshots and alerts Marshal Sam Denn, who is standing in front of Herrington & Smith's grocery store. Denn steps into the muddy street and, spying the outlaw holding the horses, opens fire on him.

The fight is on as a robber armed with a Winchester steps outside the bank and fires at the approaching townspeople, several of whom have armed themselves.

Leaving behind a sack and a pistol, the bank robbers break for their horses, but they frantically fumble with the stiff, wet reins, which won't untie easily. Finally mounting up, the outlaws gallop south out of town.

Directly across Kansas Avenue from the bank, the livery stable doors burst open and 10 cowboys explode out into the muddy street and give chase. (The cowboys were waiting out the storm in the stable before heading to a local roundup.) The instant posse overtakes the startled robbers before they even make it out of town. More shots are fired by the robbers, but the locals, led by Barney O'Connor, Vernon Lytle and Wayne McKinney, return fire and stay on the heels of the brigands.

Two and a half miles south of town, an outlaw's horse gives out. Another robber picks him up, and the outlaws ride up into a box canyon to make a stand. Quickly surrounded by the impromptu posse, the robbers hold out for several hours but give up before more reinforcements from town arrive. As the outlaws are brought back to town, the citizens are shocked to discover that all the robbers are well known in Medicine Lodge. Incredibly, two of the outlaws are lawmen from a nearby county and one of them is the Caldwell city marshal.

At the bank, cashier Geppert is found dead in the vault with two gunshot wounds, while E.W. Payne writhes on the floor from the pain of a pistol ball that entered his back near the right shoulder blade (he lives until Thursday, May 1).

Soaked and humiliated by their relatively easy capture, the outlaws are forced to pose for a photo before being thrown in the wooden jail. They will never pose for a photograph again.

★

Four riders wearing slickers approach Medicine Lodge, Kansas, as a summer thundershower overtakes them.

Inside the bank, President Payne is hit twice; one of the bullets enters behind his right shoulder blade. He dies the next day. Cashier Geppert dashes toward the safe and is fatally hit in the heart. He falls to the floor with his head just inside the vault. A clerk, F.B. Chapin, misses out on the shooting because he was at the post office.

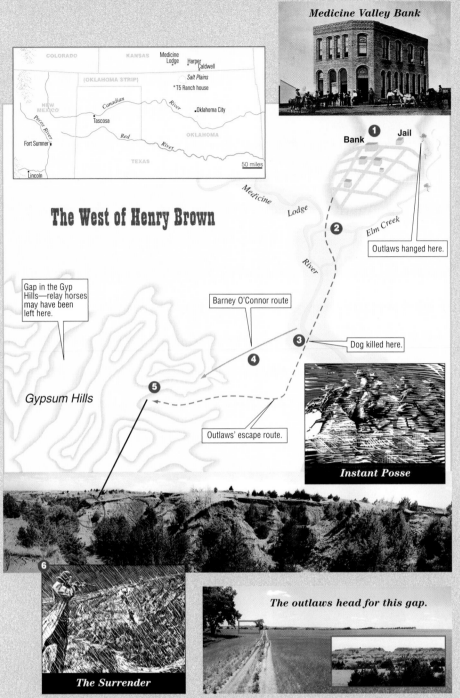

Medicine Valley Bank

The West of Henry Brown

Gap in the Gyp Hills—relay horses may have been left here.

Barney O'Connor route

Dog killed here.

Outlaws hanged here.

Bank | Jail

Gypsum Hills

Outlaws' escape route.

Instant Posse

The Surrender

The outlaws head for this gap.

Soaked and Collared Bank Robbers: *Caldwell City Marshal Henry Brown (second from left), his deputy, Ben Wheeler (far right), and two local cowboys, John Wesley (far left) and the foreman of the T5 Ranch, William Smith (in cap).*

Impending Doom

After the captors assure the robbers that they will not be mobbed, the outlaws are confronted with cries of "Hang them! Hang them!" as the posse members bring them up Main Street. Incredibly, the posse stops at a cafe to feed the suspects. After eating, the outlaws are secured with one set of leg irons and a pair of handcuffs. Brown and Wesley get the leg iron, plus their hands are tied behind them with rope; Wheeler gets his right wrist cuffed to Smith's left. The prisoners then walk to the jail, enduring strong abuse from citizens the entire way.

When the rain stops, the prisoners are escorted outside the jail for a picture (above). The photographer also takes pictures of the bank and the box canyon where the outlaws were captured.

Back in jail, the prisoners are given dry clothing and writing materials. At dusk, Henry Brown writes:

Darling Wife:—I am in jail here. Four of us tried to rob the bank here, and one man shot one of the men in the bank ... I will send you all of my things, and you can sell them, but keep the Winchester [although some disagree, this mention implies he used the special presentation Winchester in the holdup] ... we would not have been arrested, but one of our horses gave out, and we could not leave him alone.... If a mob does not kill us we will come out all right after while.

At about 9 p.m., three shots are heard, signaling citizens to join a large mob that is converging at the jail.

The Chase Down

❶ Cowboy posse explodes out of the livery stable across the street from the bank, surprising the outlaws.

❷ Henry Brown dismounts and fires several shots, trying to dissuade the locals from pursuit.

❸ The robbers cross Medicine Lodge River, where one of them fatally shoots a dog from a nearby camp.

❹ Posse man Barney O'Connor rides a borrowed nag (he was running an errand during the robbery and another posse member took his horse). He tops a rise, guesses the outlaws' destination and cuts across the open grassland, forcing the robbers into the mouth of a box canyon where they are quickly surrounded.

❺ After a futile gunfight with only slight injuries, Henry Brown yells that he will give up on the condition that he and his fellow robbers will not be mobbed. The posse members agree. Brown climbs up to a ledge (see red circle) and surrenders.

❻ As William Smith hands over his weapons, he says to his pards, "Boys, I came into it with you, and I'll go out and die with you." Truer words were never spoken.

The Newlyweds

By 1883, Henry Brown had turned his life around. After riding for several years with known outlaws, he came under the wing of a Caldwell, Kansas, family, whose members recommended him to the city as a possible lawman. Rising quickly to the position of marshal, Brown so impressed the people of Caldwell that they presented him with a custom, gold-plated Winchester rifle. In March 1884, the 26 year old married a 22-year-old local girl, Alice Maude Levagood, and bought a house. But old habits die hard. Brown asked the mayor for time off to hunt outlaws in the Oklahoma Territory and left his new bride on Sunday night, April 27. She never saw him again.

Married in Wellington, Kansas, on March 26, 1884, Henry Brown bought his new bride, Alice, a house and a milk cow.

Impromptu Cowboy Posse: (Back row, from left) Tom Doran, Barney O'Connor, Alec McKinney and Vernon Lytle. (Middle) Lee Bradley, Roll Clark (the undisputed best shot in Medicine Lodge) and Wayne McKinney. (Front) Reverend George Friedley and John Fleming. (Not pictured) Howard Martin, Nate Priest and Charlier Taliaferro. While the members of the cowboy posse are true, courageous men, they do not live up to their promise of protecting the robbers from a mob.

Hell to Pay

Three shots are heard at about 9 p.m. and several hundred men swarm the jail and sweep the guards aside. Having slipped off his boot (and the leg iron with it), Brown crouches by the door. When it swings open, he plunges into the crowd, fighting his way into the open, with Wheeler behind him. Several shots are fired at close range, but Brown, only slightly wounded, clears the crowd and makes for an open alley. A local farmer, Billy Kelley, jerks up a double-barreled shotgun and triggers both barrels, cutting Brown almost in half.

Meanwhile, Wheeler has been shot several times, and he staggers through the crowd with his vest on fire, ignited by the point-blank explosions. A bullet rips off two fingers of his left hand (above), and a Winchester ball shatters his right arm. He still makes it another 100 yards as the mob chases him and pumps bullets into him, until he falls. Incredibly, he's still alive. The mob jerks him to his feet and, along with Wesley and Smith, he is taken to the creek bottom. Wheeler whispers a confession, then adds, "Oh, men, spare my life. There's other fellows mixed up in this, and I will tell you everything if only you will spare my life."

The outlaws are asked if they have any last words. Wesley says he has a mother in Texas and requests that she not be told of his fate. Smith shows no fear and asks that his saddle be sold and the money sent to his mother, also in Texas. The three men are strung up with two ropes, with two of them (Smith and Wesley) sharing the same rope. Wheeler's bleating can be heard several blocks away. And then it's deathly quiet.

Rare Views of Medicine Lodge Bank

Thanks to collector Len Gratteri for sharing his photograph collection of the Medicine Lodge Bank. (Counter clockwise from top) An excellent view of the teller cage where Henry Brown brandished his Winchester. Looking south (behind the wagon), we see the door where the outlaws would have entered the bank. We get another view of the teller cage, and Len even found a contemporary checkbook from the bank.

R. R. Froman in his Blacksmith Shop.

R. R. FROMAN

The Henry Brown gang is surprised when a virtual swat team bursts out of the livery stable across the street from the bank. By chance, cowboys, like those directly above, were waiting out the rainstorm in the stable.

– ALL IMAGES COURTESY LEN GRATTERI COLLECTION –

After the improvised posse captures Henry Brown's gang, men congregate in various Medicine Lodge establishments, such as those above, and talk of lynching.

Wheeler's Colt

A Colt pistol attributed to Ben Wheeler as the gun he used to shoot the bank teller is now owned by Len Gratteri. Back in 1988, Gratteri began his collection of Wheeler's items when he purchased photos, Ben's assistant marshal badge and other documents from the family of Ben's wife, who had remarried and moved in 1905 to Portland, Oregon.

Henry Newton Brown (at right) circa 1879, with bravo Frederick Waite. Some historians believe the man on the right is not Brown, but John Middleton.

Aftermath: Odds & Ends

Caldwell residents were horrified by the actions of their marshal and deputy (at first they refused to believe it) but finally sent a formal apology to Medicine Lodge. A public auction was held offering the horses and saddles of the dead outlaws. Smith's saddle went for $10, the rest brought about $25 each. Wesley's gray horse got $120 and Smith's, $123.50.

⸺ ☆ ⸺

Widowed a month into her marriage, Alice Maude Levagood graduated from college, moved to Devil's Lake, North Dakota, and taught school. She also proved out a land patent, sold it to her adoptive brother and then moved to Frankfort, Indiana, where she became a nurse and a superintendent of an asylum. Late in life, she wrote a short story of her life. The only mention of her husband is that she married H.N. Brown in 1883, adding cryptically, "Mr. Brown passed away many years ago."

⸺ ☆ ⸺

Recommended: *Henry Brown: The Outlaw-Marshal* by Bill O'Neal, published by The Early West; *Meandering Medicine Lodge: The 1880's* by Beverly McCollom, self-published and available at the Stockade Museum in Medicine Lodge.

Historians speculate that after Henry's death, Alice gave his prized rifle (below, held by auctioneer Tom Keilman) to friends in Texas. It surfaced in the 1970s and was bought at auction for a reported $16,000, and later donated to the Kansas State Historical Society.

Henry Brown Rode with Billy the Kid

Henry Brown rode with the notorious Billy the Kid during the bloody Lincoln County War in New Mexico Territory (1878-1880). Henry (sometimes styled as Hendry) fought in several of the more legendary fights involving Billy the Kid, including the ambush of Sheriff Brady (see p. 32), the fight at Blazer's Mill and the climactic McSween house fight, known locally as the "Big Killing." Like the Kid, Brown bravely escaped that death trap.

He eventually landed in Tascosa, Texas, where he served briefly as a marshal and constable. But Henry Brown was a notorious hothead, states Bill O'Neal, his biographer, and the sheriff relieved Brown of his marshal duties in Tascosa because Brown "was always wanting to fight and get his mane up." Brown was also later fired from the LIT ranch "because he was always on the warpath."

After Tascosa, Brown worked for a brief time at a ranch in Woods County, Oklahoma, where his foreman was Barney O'Connor (the same cowboy who would later help capture Brown in a box canyon after the bank robbery in Medicine Lodge).

Drifting into Kansas, Brown found work as a peace officer in the wild and untamed cowtown of Caldwell, where he distinguished himself as a competent lawman.

As for Brown's mixed legacy and tragic end, one current Caldwell citizen maintains, "He was a prick when he rode with the Kid, and he died a prick."

FRIENDLY FIRE ON SNAKE ROW

☆

BILLY THOMPSON VS CHAUNCEY "CAP" WHITNEY

☆

"GET YOUR GUNS, YOU TEXAS SONS-OF-BITCHES AND FIGHT!"

☆

Billy Thompson lets loose on the wrong man.

AUGUST 15, 1873

Big Ben Thompson walks up to gambler John Sterling in Nick Lentz's Saloon on Snake Row in Ellsworth, Kansas. He asks for "his fair cut" from a game of Monte just finished. In his cups, Sterling strikes Ben across the face. As a fight breaks out, policeman "Happy Jack" Morco, who was talking with Sterling when Ben approached, pulls two revolvers and forces Ben to back off. Grabbing Sterling, Morco guides him out of the saloon.

Ben goes back to Brennan's Saloon (site of the original Monte game) and is telling a Texan friend about his altercation when a shout from outside is heard: "Get your guns, you Texas sons-of-bitches and fight!" It is Happy Jack Morco, with two drawn pistols, and Sterling armed with a shotgun.

Ben begs his friends to loan him a firearm but they refuse, so he ducks out the back door of Brennan's and makes for Jake New's place, where he checked his guns earlier. Stuffing his revolver in his belt, Ben loads his Winchester and steps out onto S. Main Street. As he does, his very drunk older brother, Billy, joins him, having grabbed Ben's double-barreled shotgun.

Cocking both barrels, Billy staggers. Just as Ben warns him to be careful, one of the barrels goes off, striking the sidewalk in front of New's saloon, at the feet of Texas drovers Seth Mabry and Eugene Millett.

Ben grabs the shotgun away from his brother and tries to extract the shells, but they are brass and swollen. He hands the shotgun to someone else and steps into the street. Determined to make a stand with his brother, Billy retrieves the shotgun and follows Ben. Looking down Snake Row to where Sterling and Morco are standing, Ben bellows, "If you sons-of-bitches want to fight us, here we are!"

Across the plaza, on the opposite side of the tracks, Sheriff Chauncey B. Whitney is enjoying a meal with John "Long Jack" DeLong at Veatch's Hotel and Restaurant. The sheriff stayed in town instead of going on a picnic with his family. The sister of his wife, Nellie Henry, was being courted by John Montgomery, editor of the *Ellsworth Reporter*, who had informed the sheriff that he may want to stick around because Billy was on a bender that day.

Hearing the report of the shotgun, the unarmed sheriff leaves the restaurant, with DeLong behind him. Stepping across the tracks, he calls out, "Boys, don't have any row. I will do all I can to protect you. You know John and I are your friends."

Trying to calm down the Thompson brothers, the sheriff offers, "Come let us go to Brennan's and take a drink." Both Whitney and Ben ask Billy to let down the hammers on the shotgun, but Billy will not comply, saying, "I'm not going to let those damn sons-of-bitches get the best of Ben." He does, however, promise to ease off the hammers once he reaches the saloon.

Walking across the plaza, the men reach Brennan's. As they enter, a Texas stockman, W.A. Langford, yells out a warning that Morco is advancing down the boardwalk with a pistol in each hand. Ben spins around, brings his Winchester up to his shoulder and fires at the rapidly approaching Morco, who dives into the entrance of Beebe's General Store. The bullet hits the door casing, missing Morco.

Coming out on the boardwalk, Sheriff Whitney steps forward, asking, "What does all this mean?" Behind the sheriff, Billy staggers out of the saloon. As he tries to recover himself, the shotgun goes off, striking the sheriff in the right side (chest area).

"Oh, I am shot!" Whitney cries, as Ben Thompson screams, "My God, Billy, you have shot our best friend!"

Billy recovers, saying sheepishly, "I am sorry."

Bystanders crowd around the mortally-wounded sheriff, who says, "He did not mean it. It was accidental, send for my wife and baby."

The fight that never came off is over, but this is where a dubious legend begins.

ELLSWORTH, KANSAS

Founded six years before the Thompson brothers arrived, the town of Ellsworth was only a whistle stop on the Kansas Pacific Railroad (K.P.R.R.) line and looked to remain one until angry farmers pushed the cattle droves west of Abilene. A significant number of Texas cattlemen found Ellsworth a welcome shipping point in both 1871 and 1872. The K.P.R.R. prepared for the 1873 season by upgrading the holding pens and adding more loading chutes on the west side of town. The facility could now load 200 boxcars of cattle per day.

The summer of 1873 saw the Thompson brothers in Ellsworth. While Billy was primarily a cowboy, Ben set up a gambling gig in Brennan's Saloon, which gave him a percentage of the take.

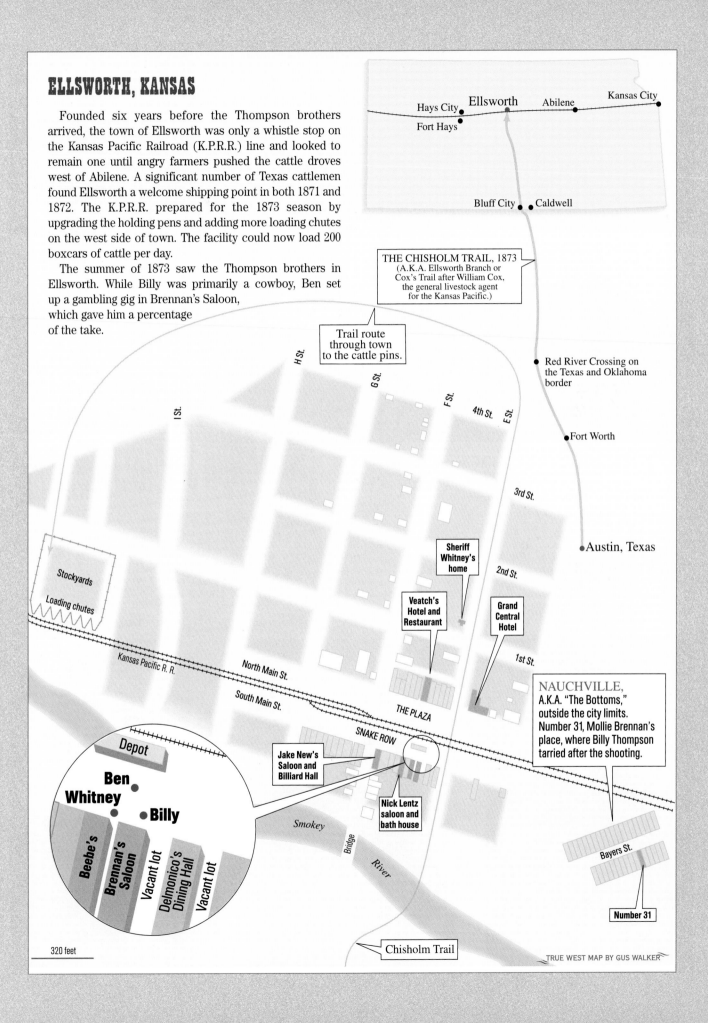

THE CHISHOLM TRAIL, 1873
(A.K.A. Ellsworth Branch or Cox's Trail after William Cox, the general livestock agent for the Kansas Pacific.)

Trail route through town to the cattle pins.

Hays City
Ellsworth
Abilene
Kansas City
Fort Hays
Bluff City Caldwell

Red River Crossing on the Texas and Oklahoma border

Fort Worth

Austin, Texas

H St.
G St.
F St.
4th St.
E St.
3rd St.
2nd St.
1st St.
1st.

Sheriff Whitney's home

Veatch's Hotel and Restaurant

Grand Central Hotel

Stockyards

Loading chutes

Kansas Pacific R. R.

North Main St.

South Main St.

THE PLAZA

SNAKE ROW

NAUCHVILLE, A.K.A. "The Bottoms," outside the city limits. Number 31, Mollie Brennan's place, where Billy Thompson tarried after the shooting.

Jake New's Saloon and Billiard Hall

Nick Lentz saloon and bath house

Depot

Ben Whitney

Billy

Beebe's

Brennan's Saloon

Vacant lot

Delmonico's Dining Hall

Vacant lot

Smokey

Bridge

River

Bayers St.

Number 31

320 feet

Chisholm Trail

TRUE WEST MAP BY GUS WALKER

Brennan's Saloon

Grand Hotel

Ellsworth, Kansas, 1873, as it looked at the time of the fight. Below that photo is one showing the same site in 2003. None of the original buildings in the top photo remain. The Grand Hotel burned in the 1960s and was demolished.

– BOTTOM PHOTO BY NATALIE BICKNELL –

A Hefty Reward Went Unclaimed

Although a large reward was offered (at right), Billy Thompson was never brought to justice. Immediately after the fight, Billy was given a horse, a pistol and some cash by his Texan friends as his brother told him, "For God's sake leave town." Instead, Billy rode to Nauchville (see map, previous page) to visit brothel owner Mollie Brennan; he allegedly "partook of her charms."

GOVERNOR'S PROCLAMATION.

WHEREAS, C. B. Whitney, Sheriff of Ellsworth County, Kansas, was murdered in the said county of Ellsworth, on the 15th day of August, 1873, by one William Thompson, said Thompson being described as about six feet in height, 26 years of age, dark complexion, brown hair, gray eyes and erect form; and Whereas, the said William Thompson is now at large and a fugitive from justice;

NOW THEREFORE, know ye, that I, Thomas A. Osborn, Governor of the State of Kansas, in pursuance of law, do hereby offer a reward of FIVE HUNDRED DOLLARS for the arrest and conviction of the said William Thompson, for the crime above named.

L. S.

IN TESTIMONY WHEREOF, I have hereunto subscribed my name, and caused to be affixed the Great Seal of the State. Done at Topeka, this 22d day of August, 1873.

By the Governor:

THOMAS A. OSBORN.

W. H. SMALLWOOD, Secretary of State.

Ben Thompson

Billy Thompson

Sheriff Chauncey Whitney

Did Wyatt Earp Disarm Ben Thompson?

Late in life, Wyatt Earp (left) told his biographer Stuart Lake that he watched with disgust as Billy Thompson rode out of town after killing Sheriff Whitney. Earp said he accepted the city marshal badge from Mayor James Miller and borrowed a pair of used six-guns from Beebe's General Store. Then he boldly walked across the Plaza, under the guns of countless Texans, and placed Ben Thompson under arrest, ending the standoff and preventing further bloodshed.

Before the 1931 publication of *Wyatt Earp: Frontier Marshal*, not one word about Earp's involvement was ever published. The *Ellsworth Reporter*, the town's sole newspaper, reported extensively on the shooting and its aftermath, yet it never mentioned Earp. Earp's alleged arrest of Ben was never mentioned in the paper's reports of Billy's nine-day trial, nor was Earp on the trial's witness list. And the minutes of Ellsworth's city council meetings didn't have an entry stating Earp was sworn in.

Earp worshippers still trot out the venerable old-timers who, being interviewed after the publication of the book, suddenly remembered Wyatt being there.

Of all the Earp claims, this one is the most dubious.

Four Jacks and a Joker

"Nobody Killed Yet" proclaimed the *Ellsworth Reporter* in its July 3, 1873, issue. With the Texas cattle season in full swing, the editor and the residents of Ellsworth were beaming proud, or perhaps just nervously optimistic.

The police force consisted of City Marshal "Brocky Jack" Norton, John "Long Jack" DeLong, John "Happy Jack" Morco, John "High Low Jack" Brauham and Edward Hogue (who also served double duty as a deputy sheriff). Local wags referred to them as "Four Jacks and a Joker."

Years later, an old-timer recalled them all as "... scoundrels. Every man on the force was a bribe-taker and a villain. Every man

on the force would kill on the slightest provocation, if he felt his hide was safe in doing so, every man on the force in those days would not hesitate to commit any crime, in order to satisfy his passions."

By most accounts, Morco was a swaggering illiterate, a self-described Indian fighter and gunman, who claimed to have shot a dozen men. In June, Morco arrested Billy Thompson for assaulting him, carrying a deadly weapon and disturbing the peace (it was Billy's second arrest and he paid a heavy fine). Morco definitely reserved a special hatred for the Thompson brothers, which came out that day on Snake Row.

Aftermath: Odds & Ends

Having lost his pistol and money after sleeping off a visit with Mollie Brennan (see p. 16), Billy Thompson rode back into town, where his younger brother Ben and others dressed him as a vaquero and snuck him out to a cattle outfit, back to Texas. With a $500 reward on his head, Billy remained on the dodge for three years until the Texas Rangers rounded him up. He was extradited to Kansas, declared not guilty in 1877 and returned to Texas. His name doesn't crop up again until the summer of 1880, when he gets in a shoot-out with Texan Jim Tucker in Ogallala, Nebraska.

⸺ ☆ ⸺

Sheriff Chauncey Whitney suffered in agony for three days, dying on August 18. His body was buried under Masonic honors in the Episcopal Church cemetery, within sight of the backyard of his house.

⸺ ☆ ⸺

Ben Thompson's 12-gauge, breech loading, centerfire shotgun was a gift from Texas cowboy Cad Pierce. Ironically, an Ellsworth police officer shot and beat Pierce to death two days after the Whitney shooting, when Pierce confronted lawmen about rumors of all Texans being ordered out of town. Ben eventually pawned the shotgun to Chalk Beeson of Dodge City for $75. (Today, the scattergun is prominently displayed at Front Street's Boot Hill Museum in Dodge City.) Ben's next brush with the law doesn't take place until Christmas night in 1876 when a fight erupts at a theatre in Austin, Texas.

⸺ ☆ ⸺

Two Ellsworth policemen were killed not long after the fight: "Happy Jack" Morco, fatally shot by J. Charles Brown (who later became a city marshal), and Edward Crawford, gunned down by a Texas cowboy, who allegedly may have been Cad's brother-in-law (Crawford was the lawman who had beaten Cad to death).

⸺ ☆ ⸺

Recommended: Jim Gray's *Kansas Cowboy*, official publication of the C.O.W.B.O.Y. Society.

TRAGIC POWWOW

⸺ ☆ ⸺

THE APACHE KID VS AL SIEBER, THEN EVERYONE IN ARIZONA

⸺ ☆ ⸺

A miscommunication changes the Apache Kid's life.

JUNE 1, 1887

Absent from duty for five days, the Apache Kid, along with four other Apache scouts under his command, ride single file into the headquarters of the San Carlos Reservation (near Globe, Arizona). The Kid was acting chief of scouts while Al Sieber was away at Fort Apache and the White River Subagency.

Upon his return to San Carlos, Sieber has summoned the Kid after hearing he killed another Apache in an alcohol-fueled family feud. (The offending liquor? Tizwin, a traditional Apache drink made from the heart of the mescal plant.)

Told by a messenger that the Kid wants to powwow, Sieber contacts the commanding officer, Capt. Francis Pierce; two interpreters are also notified. The clock is approaching 5 p.m. as Sieber and Pierce proceed, on foot, from headquarters to Sieber's tent (a 75-yard walk) to meet the incoming party.

Despite the appearance of the Kid and his men, who are carrying their arms openly in direct violation of camp regulations, none of the men in Sieber's party is armed.

As word of the scouts' arrival has spread, other Apaches from the nearby camps are gravitating toward the tent, and some of them are armed, as well.

Walking up to the scouts, Sieber says, "Hello Kid." Returning the greeting, the Apache Kid and his scouts dismount, with their weapons in their hands.

Captain Pierce asks, "Where are the five scouts who have been absent?" The Apache Kid and the others step forward.

"Give me your rifle," Pierce orders the Kid. The Kid complies. Pierce demands his gun belt, too, and the Kid gives it up. The captain places the rifle against Sieber's tent and the gun belt in a chair. He then demands the same from the other four scouts. They, in turn, give up their arms and gun belts.

Pointing in the direction of the guardhouse, the captain barks, "Calaboose!" (Spanglish for jail). Several of the Indians pick up their gun belts and remove their knife scabbards.

At this point, both Pierce and Sieber hear an "unusual commotion." They turn to see mounted Indians loading their rifles. (The assembled Apaches later claim one of the interpreters, Antonio Diaz, had intimated, with Apache sign, that the arrested scouts would be sent to the "island," which signified Alcatraz or even Florida, where Geronimo and other Apache leaders were being held as prisoners of war; see quote, opposite page.)

> Pointing in the direction of the guardhouse, the captain barks, "Calaboose!". . . At this point, both Pierce and Sieber hear an "unusual commotion."

Alarmed by this prospect, several of the disarmed scouts lunge for their weapons as Capt. Pierce jumps in between them, trying to shove their guns away and out of reach. The Kid makes a grab for his carbine, but Sieber grabs the rifle with his right hand, while shoving the Kid back with his left.

Unable to retrieve his weapon, the Kid runs around the tent and disappears.

"Look out, Sieber!" Pierce yells, "They are going to shoot!" Sieber kicks the guns toward the tent as two shots ring out, one right after the other. Sieber and Pierce dive into the tent as bullets rip through the twin openings, from front to back.

Sieber grabs his weapon and runs out to engage the shooters. He fires at a mounted Apache who has just fired at him. But before Sieber can fire again, a .45-70 slug tears into his left leg below the knee, breaking the bone and knocking him flat. He crawls back into the tent as the Apaches disappear into the twilight.

The unexpected gunfight is over, but the long, tragic nightmare of the Apache Kid has just begun.

★

> "The Indians know by motions. We know by signs. Antonio reached out his hand and made a circle in his hand and spoke in Apache at the same time. He said that the five scouts will be sent down to the islands."
>
> —*Chief Gonshayee, an eyewitness to the fight, who testifies that Antonio Diaz's sign conveyed to the Indians that the scouts would be sent to Alcatraz or Florida, which triggers the shoot-out*

Chief of Scouts Al Sieber is crippled for life after his leg stops a .45-70 slug during the Apache Kid melee.

– ALL PHOTOS TRUE WEST ARCHIVES –

Caught Between the Military and the Deep Blue Sea

Two companies of cavalry take the field within 15 minutes of the fight. They trail the Apaches for 15 miles along the San Carlos River (the Kid's party includes about 17 members; some are on foot, as they were unable to find a horse in time). From the river, the fleeing Apaches turn south, through Aravaipa Canyon.

When the Apaches reach the San Pedro River, one of the renegades, believed to be a Yaqui, kills William Diehl near Mammoth Mill, 60 miles north of Benson. The band steals two horses and then strikes again, killing Mike Grace, whose body is found northwest of Crittenden.

After a feint toward Mexico, the Kid's band camps high on the Rincon Mountains (east of Tucson), where soldiers surprise them, capturing all of the Apaches' horses and supplies.

After 24 days of running, the Kid surrenders. He is then tried, along with four scouts, by a military court.

The Kid and his scouts are found guilty and sentenced to death by firing squad, but Gen. Nelson Miles objects to the ruling and asks the court to reconsider its verdict.

On August 3, at Camp Thomas, the reconvened court resentences the five to life imprisonment, which Miles reduces to 10 years. Under heavy guard, the convicted scouts, including the Kid, are delivered to Alcatraz, in San Francisco Bay, to serve their time.

Upon military review of the case, which reveals prejudice among officers on the jury, the Apache Kid's sentence is overturned, and he is sent home after serving 16 months.

Angry Arizona civilians convince the courts that the military had no jurisdiction in the case. By the close of 1888, the Kid and his comrades have been ordered back to San Carlos.

A new trial is held in Globe, and Al Sieber is the chief witness against the Apaches. Not surprisingly, the jury declares all the defendants guilty and the judge sentences them to seven years in Yuma Territorial Prison.

The Apache Kid and other prisoners are gathered for transport to Yuma, via Riverside and the rail station in Casa Grande. Al Sieber offers Sheriff Glenn Reynolds the use of an army escort, but the sheriff declines. It costs him his life.

A Daring Escape!

November 1, 1889

It is a rough, two-day stage ride from Globe to Casa Grande, Arizona. Sheriff Glenn Reynolds is transporting the Apache Kid and eight other prisoners who will be put on the train in Casa Grande to take them to the Yuma penitentiary. The weather is cold and wet, and snow is in the forecast.

On the second morning, four miles out of Riverside (see map, below), the stage encounters Ripsey Wash, followed by a steep incline. The sheriff and his hired guard, William "Hunkydory" Holmes, get out of the stage, along with seven of the prisoners. With only the driver, Eugene Middleton, and two prisoners aboard (including the Kid), the horses struggle but successfully make it up the soggy and steepest part of the ridge. It is snowing.

As Middleton and his coach clear the grade, he hears men scuffling behind him, then two shots (at first he's not alarmed because the sheriff had been target shooting earlier). When Middleton looks back, though, he can't see anything through the brush.

In a moment, a Mexican prisoner, Jesus Avott, frantically runs up, explaining that the Indians are going to kill him. He asks Middleton what to do, and the driver tells him to get on the stage. As Avott raises his foot to get in, one of the Apache prisoners, Bach-e-on-al, runs up, brandishing Holmes' rifle. He fires, hitting Middleton in the face, and the driver topples to the ground. The newly freed prisoners bring up the keys and unchain the Kid as they debate whether to crush Middleton's skull with a rock (popular legend says the Apache Kid stops them because Middleton had shared a cigarette with the Kid the night before at Riverside Station).

Grabbing ammunition, money and whatever else they can use, the escapees cut loose the horses and scatter into the wilderness.

Incredibly, Middleton is still alive and makes his way back toward Riverside for help.

A subsequent posse is thwarted by a snowstorm that obliterates the fugitives' tracks.

The stage road from Riverside to Florence follows several washes like this one, at right, which drains into Ripsey Wash. This steep stretch is about 50 yards shy of the ambush site; it would have been difficult for a stage full of prisoners to traverse this area in wet conditions. Below is a panorama taken of the spot where Middleton stopped the stage. Notice that he wouldn't have been able to see around the bushes that flank the road leading into the draw.

Ridge topping out from Kelvin Grade (arrow); Spot where Middleton rested the horses (X).

The Prisoners' Perfect Moment

Trudging up the steep grade (left), Sheriff Reynolds is walking in front of the prisoners. He carries a shotgun over his arm, but his pistol and gun belt is stored under his long coat, which is buttoned up against the cold. When two of the Indians rush the sheriff, they quickly overpower him by pinning his arms. Meanwhile, the two Apaches walking in front of Holmes, who is bringing up the rear, turn and throw a blanket they are carrying over his head. They grab Holmes' rifle from him and fatally shoot Reynolds; Holmes dies of a heart attack.

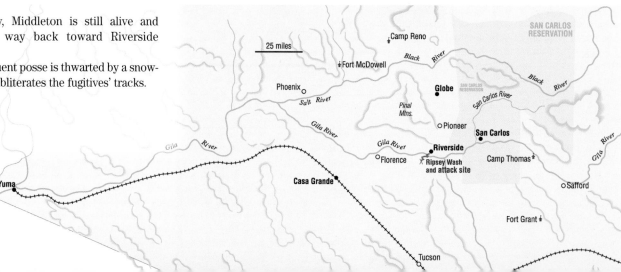

The Prisoners are Photographed Prior to Their Bold Escape

After a group of Apache defendants is found guilty in a Globe courtroom, they are photographed (above) before they depart for the Yuma Territorial Prison. Note that the Apache Kid (standing, second from right) is still wearing his brass reservation tag on his left breast pocket.

When the Apaches get out of the stage near Ripsey Wash, Bach-e-on-al (front row, center, indicted under the name Pash-ten-tah) allegedly slips free of his handcuffs. He and El-cahn (standing, far left) overpower the sheriff as another two Apaches attack Holmes, who reportedly dies of a heart attack before being shot. Hos-cal-te and Say-es (standing, second and third from left) are later recaptured and die in prison. Not shown is prisoner Jesus Avott, sentenced to one year in prison for selling a friend's horse for $50.

The Fallen Lawmen

While transporting the prisoners via stage, Sheriff Reynolds (right) carried a Colt .45 and a double-barreled shotgun loaded with buckshot. In addition to turning down the offer of a scout escort (Reynolds allegedly told Al Sieber "I can take those Indians alone with a corncob and a lightning bug."), the sheriff started the trip with his horse, which he left at Riverside. Had he been on horseback, he may have averted the disastrous outcome.

Hunkydory Holmes (bottom right) had a lever action Winchester and a pistol. Middleton also carried a pistol. On the ill-fated journey, Holmes allegedly took it upon himself to cheer up the prisoners by sharing his original poetry. Here's a few lines:

Hunkydory
Oh, I am a jolly miner lad,
Resolved to see some fun sir,
To satisfy my mind
To Phoenix town I came sir
Oh, what a pretty place
And what a charming city
Where the boys they are so gay
And the squaws they are so pretty

Aftermath: Odds & Ends

Military and civilian authorities launched a colossal manhunt for the escapees. By the summer of 1890, all the fugitives had been killed or captured—all except the Apache Kid. By 1892, the State of Arizona offered a $6,000 reward for the Kid, and several officers were commanded to bring in the Kid, dead or alive. No one ever claimed the reward.

☆

Eugene Middleton survived his face wounds and ran the Riverside stage station for several years. He then moved to Globe where he owned a successful apartment building. He died in 1929 of natural causes. He was 68.

☆

Some historians believe that the Kid escaped into the Sierra Madre Mountains in Old Mexico where he lived out his life.

☆

In 1937, a Norwegian explorer and anthropologist, Helge Ingstad, heard that renegade Apaches still lived in Mexico. Traveling deep into the Sierra Madres, Ingstad claimed he found a woman, Lupe, who was thought to be the daughter of the Apache Kid.

Recommended: *The Apache Kid* by Phyllis de la Garza, published by Westernlore Press; *Al Sieber: Chief of Scouts* by Dan L. Thrapp, published by University of Oklahoma Press.

To the Apaches, the Kid was known as Has-kay-bay-nay-ntayl, which means "brave and tall and will come to a mysterious end." Quite a fitting name, since we don't know what happened to him.

TUMBLING DICE
EARNS HARDIN A ONE-WAY TICKET TO HELL

JOHN WESLEY HARDIN VS CONSTABLE JOHN SELMAN

A MISTRESS NAMED M'ROSE IS THE CAUSE

Constable John Selman steps through the swinging doors of the Acme Saloon.

Wes Hardin is drunk and furious. "I'll go and get a gun," he bellows at John Selman, Sr., "and when I meet you, I'll meet you smoking, and make you shit like a wolf around the block!" The two part ways.

> "The last words he spoke before the first shot were 'Four sixes to beat,' and they were addressed to me."
>
> —*H.S. Brown*

Later that night, Hardin is standing at the bar, just inside the front door of the Acme Saloon in El Paso, Texas, rolling dice for drinks with a local grocer. According to the clock on the wall, it is the eleventh hour, but for the aging gunfighter, the seconds are ticking to eternity.

"It was a hot night," Patrick McGeeney later testifies, "sultry, with heavy humidity." Two old cattlemen are seated at a nearby table in the smoky din, relating their adventures with Cochise, Geronimo, John Ringo, Pat Garrett and Billy the Kid.

"Hoss piss on you," bellows Hardin, grumbling at the ivory numerical combinations on the bar.

"Shake again," the grocer grunts.

"You have four sixes to beat," says Hardin, as the dice tumble to a stop on the hardwood bar top.

Stepping through the swinging doors, John Selman, Sr. fires his pistol. The bullet enters the back of Hardin's head, exits above his left eye and hits the mirror behind the bar, shattering it. Crumpling to the floor, Hardin falls face up. Selman steps over him and fires three more times, hitting Hardin in the chest and taking the tip off the gunfighter's pinkie on his left hand.

As patrons clamber for the exits, Constable John Selman, Jr. runs in and grabs his dad's arm, saying, "Don't shoot anymore! He's dead!"

That's how Hardin died. But the bigger question is why?

Selman's Self-Serving Version

"I met Wes Hardin about 7 o'clock last evening close to the Acme Saloon. When we met, Hardin said: 'You've got a son that's a bastardly, cowardly son of a bitch!' I said, 'Which one?' Hardin said: 'John, the one that's on the police force. He pulled my woman when I was absent and robbed her of $50, which they wouldn't have done, if I had been here.' I said: 'Hardin; there is no man on earth that can talk about my children like that without fighting, you cowardly son of a bitch!' Hardin said: 'I am unarmed.' I said: 'Go and get your gun; I am armed.' Then he said: 'I'll go and get a gun and when I meet you, I'll meet you smoking, and make you shit like a wolf around the block.'

I said he'd be the first man that ever did. About 11 o'clock I came into the Acme saloon to take a drink with Mr. Shackelford. Shackelford said to come in and take a drink with him but not to go to getting drunk. I told him I would not get drunk for I expected trouble. Hardin threw his hand on his gun and I grabbed mine and went to shooting. He threw his hand back on a gun in his hip pocket before I pulled and went to shooting."

In the 1870s, Wes Hardin is known as Texas' most notorious man killer.

May You Be Found Among Lawyers

John Wesley Hardin as he appears in El Paso near the end of his life.

Out of prison a mere 18 months, John Wesley Hardin has landed in a strange, new world. His children are grown, with families of their own. He suffers constant pain from numerous old wounds; the buffalo are gone—not to mention the Daltons, Jesse James and Billy the Kid— the great cattle drives are ancient history and in fact, many of the cowtowns Hardin hurrahed in his heyday are now cities. To make matters worse, Hardin is now an attorney, summing up the old gypsy curse: may you be found among lawyers.

For a time after his release from prison in February 1894, Hardin stayed away from saloons and gambling halls, but a disastrous 10-day marriage to a young, flirtatious teenager has left him depressed and embittered. He has gradually returned, with a vengeance, to the life he had sworn to forsake. To boot, a disastrous run for sheriff in Gonzales, Texas, has sent the aging ex-gunfighter tumbling westward.

The *El Paso Times* welcomed the well-known shootist, reporting that "forty-one years [has] steadied the impetuous cowboy down to a peaceable, dignified quiet man of business."

Hardin, who probably paid for the kind newspaper comments, is hanging onto his peaceable dignity by his fingernails. He will not hang long.

Hardin's law office is located on the second floor, immediately to the right of the center telephone pole in front of the Wells Fargo Building.

– COURTESY STATE NATIONAL BANK COLLECTION –

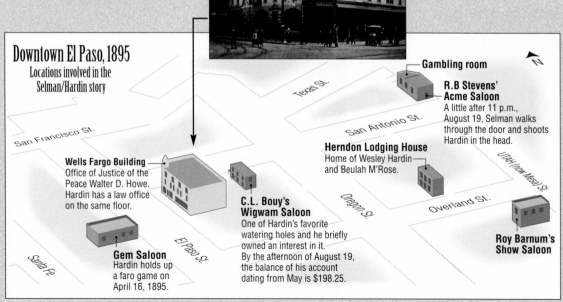

Downtown El Paso, 1895
Locations involved in the Selman/Hardin story

N

Gambling room

R.B Stevens' Acme Saloon
A little after 11 p.m., August 19, Selman walks through the door and shoots Hardin in the head.

Herndon Lodging House
Home of Wesley Hardin and Beulah M'Rose.

Wells Fargo Building
Office of Justice of the Peace Walter D. Howe. Hardin has a law office on the same floor.

C.L. Bouy's Wigwam Saloon
One of Hardin's favorite watering holes and he briefly owned an interest in it. By the afternoon of August 19, the balance of his account dating from May is $198.25.

Gem Saloon
Hardin holds up a faro game on April 16, 1895.

Roy Barnum's Show Saloon

Texas St.
San Antonio St.
San Francisco St.
Oregon St.
Overland St.
UTAH (now Mesa) St.
El Paso St.
Santa Fe

A Shady Lady & A Murky Murder

In early April 1895, Attorney Wes Hardin is approached by a sexy, ex-prostitute—Mrs. Beulah M'Rose—who tells a woeful border tale of injustice and wrongful arrest. Her Polish cowboy husband, Martin M'Rose, has been jailed in Juarez, Mexico, where the authorities took some $1,800 in cash from her, which she maintains is from the legitimate sale of her husband's cattle ranch near Eddy, New Mexico.

Hardin agrees to take her case. He immediately retains a Mexican lawyer and talks to the American consul in Juarez. After Hardin spreads around sufficient cash, the Mexican Supreme Court orders the release of Martin and a friend. Both remain in Juarez, awaiting naturalization papers.

In addition to taking the case, Hardin also takes his vivacious client to bed. While in bed, the counselor advises Mrs. M'Rose not to send additional money to her husband (a reported $3,400).

Martin is not happy on hearing this and is intent on getting back his wife, or at least his money. Unfortunately, he's wanted for rustling in the U.S. and has a $250 price on his head. In Juarez, Martin confers with U.S. Deputy Marshal George Scarborough, who agrees to meet the cuckolded husband in the middle of the international bridge separating Juarez from El Paso and escort him to a secret rendezvous with his estranged wife. Martin walks directly into an ambush and is shot dead by U.S. Deputy Marshal Jeff Milton, Texas Ranger Frank McMahan and, some say, Constable John Selman, Sr.

The lawmen claim they killed Martin for the reward, but rumors circulate that Hardin had the most to gain from the death; he likely planned the assassination and paid the gunmen. Hardin, while drunk, admitted as much, bragging he paid Scarborough to kill Martin. Enraged, Scarborough forced Hardin to accompany him to a newspaper office to dictate a retraction. Hardin complied meekly.

When Hardin went out of town on business, Beulah got drunk and combative. Disarmed, she was arrested and thrown in jail by Constable John Selman, Jr. "Old" John Selman claimed this arrest sparked the fight between himself and Hardin.

A Rowdy Fraternity of Deadly Man Killers

In El Paso, Wes Hardin mingles with a vicious set of men who thrive beneath the dark underbelly of the West's rowdiest border town. Only one of them lives to old age.

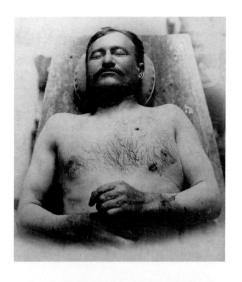

*Martin M'Rose
as he appears in the morgue.*

El Paso Chief of Police Jeff Milton (left) and U.S. Deputy George Scarborough, circa 1895. Although the two are known for their bravery, the M'Rose affair taints their careers.

– COURTESY HALEY LIBRARY IN MIDLAND, TEXAS –

Mrs. M'Rose

El Paso constable John Selman, Jr. arrests a drunken Beulah M'Rose and sets the wheels turning for the showdown.

John Wesley Hardin: A Vicious and Violent Life

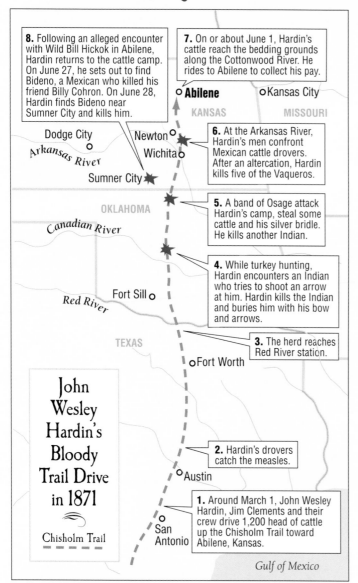

8. Following an alleged encounter with Wild Bill Hickok in Abilene, Hardin returns to the cattle camp. On June 27, he sets out to find Bideno, a Mexican who killed his friend Billy Cohron. On June 28, Hardin finds Bideno near Sumner City and kills him.

7. On or about June 1, Hardin's cattle reach the bedding grounds along the Cottonwood River. He rides to Abilene to collect his pay.

○ Abilene   ○ Kansas City

KANSAS   MISSOURI

Dodge City ○   Newton ○

Arkansas River   Wichita ○

Sumner City

6. At the Arkansas River, Hardin's men confront Mexican cattle drovers. After an altercation, Hardin kills five of the Vaqueros.

OKLAHOMA

Canadian River

5. A band of Osage attack Hardin's camp, steal some cattle and his silver bridle. He kills another Indian.

Fort Sill ○

Red River

4. While turkey hunting, Hardin encounters an Indian who tries to shoot an arrow at him. Hardin kills the Indian and buries him with his bow and arrows.

TEXAS

3. The herd reaches Red River station.

○ Fort Worth

John Wesley Hardin's Bloody Trail Drive in 1871

Chisholm Trail
- - - - -

2. Hardin's drovers catch the measles.

○ Austin

1. Around March 1, John Wesley Hardin, Jim Clements and their crew drive 1,200 head of cattle up the Chisholm Trail toward Abilene, Kansas.

○ San Antonio

Gulf of Mexico

Historians believe Hardin killed approximately 20-50 men. Every life event seemed an opportunity for carnage (a cattle drive produced eight corpses, see above). By the time he reaches El Paso, he is due some bad karma, and he gets it at the Acme Saloon (below).

John Wesley Hardin, already an established killer at age 18.

May 26, 1853

John Wesley Hardin is born in Bonhom, Texas. At age 15, he kills his first man, Freedman "Mage" Holshousen.

January 9, 1871

Hardin is arrested in Longview, Texas, and charged with horse theft and four counts of murder. By now, he has murdered eight men. On his way to Waco to stand trial, he kills a guard and escapes.

February 29, 1872

Hardin marries 14-year-old Jane Bowen. They have three children together, but he is rarely home.

October 5, 1878

After killing some two dozen men (Hardin claims 27), he enters prison in Huntsville, Texas, where he has been sentenced to serve 25 years of hard labor.

February 17, 1894

After serving almost 16 years, Hardin is released. He walks out of prison a widower with three grown children. He also has a law degree.

August 19, 1895

Constantly drunk, Hardin makes threats against John Selman, Jr., and John's father, Selman, Sr. guns down Hardin in the Acme Saloon. He was 42.

As John Selman re-enters the Acme Saloon, he pulls his pistol, takes a step or two and fires point-blank into the back of Hardin's head.

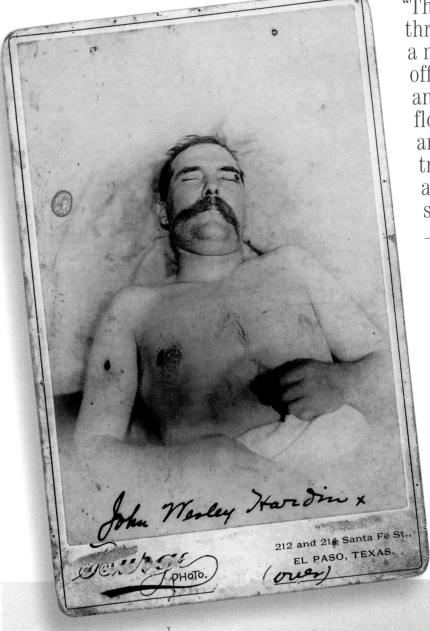

John Wesley Hardin ×

212 and 21? Santa Fe St.,
EL PASO, TEXAS.

George PHOTO.

(over)

"The bullet that passed through Hardin's head struck a mirror frame and glanced off and fell in front of the bar and the lower end. In the floor where Hardin fell there are three bullet holes in triangle shape and about a span apart. They range straight through the floor."

—*R.B. Stevens, owner of the Acme Saloon*

After Hardin is killed, his body is removed to the undertakers, who clean and prepare it for photographing and burial.

Disguised as a Mexican, M'Rose is ambushed as he and U.S. Deputy George Scarborough (running out of the line of fire, lower right) traverse a dump on the U.S. side of the border.

Hardin's Scars: The Undertaker's Tally

"Starr Undertakers removed the body, and during an examination at the mortuary, they recorded numerous scars. Two side-by-side gunshot wounds were above the right hip bone. The left thigh midway between the knee and the groin had a gunshot wound, and a similar abrasion existed on the inside of the right thigh. A wound glistened on the back of the right elbow, and a large knife scar with several adjoining smaller scars appeared below the rib on the left side."

—Leon Metz, in his book:
John Wesley Hardin: Dark Angel of Texas

Hardin was fond of shooting holes in playing cards, signing them— sometimes dating them—and giving them away as mementos. He may also have sold them to raise money for his drinking and gambling.

Aftermath: Odds & Ends

At his murder trial, John Selman, Sr. testified he was actually in the Acme Saloon prior to the shooting, sitting at a table with a friend. He said John Wesley Hardin had been watching him in the mirror behind the bar and claimed (or at least implied) that Hardin was waiting for an opportunity to kill him. Selman said he then went outside to talk to a friend who advised him not to get drunk. When they turned to go back inside, Selman suddenly pulled his pistol and shot Hardin from behind.

As to a motive beyond the threats, some historians speculate Hardin paid the other Martin M'Rose shooters, but he didn't pay Selman, and that error led to the shooting.

Yet Hardin biographer Leon Metz is blunt about the why of it: "When it comes right down to it, we don't really know why Selman shot and killed Hardin. We do know that Selman and Hardin argued in the street shortly before Hardin's death, but about what, we don't know."

As with many of the Old West shoot-outs, while we may never know the true cause, the deadly mixture of liquor, guns, pride and threats was usually more than enough fuel for the fire.

Beulah M'Rose fled El Paso prior to Hardin's death and ended up in Phoenix, Arizona, where she disappeared from history.

Selman's first trial ended with a hung jury. Before his next court date, however, he was killed by none other than George Scarborough, but that's another *Classic Gunfight.*

Recommended: *John Wesley Hardin: Dark Angel of Texas* by Leon Metz, published by Mangan Press.

WILD BILL'S LAST FIGHT

WILD BILL HICKOK VS PHIL COE

A TRAGIC TURN, THE PRINCE OF THE PISTOLEERS IS TOO GOOD FOR HIS OWN GOOD

A successful season goes south for Wild Bill Hickok.

OCTOBER 5, 1871

Wild Bill returns fire, mortally wounding gambler Phil Coe in front of the Alamo Saloon. News reports claim at least 50 cowboys were gathered on the street at the time of the shooting; the reports imply that several were injured by ricochet bullets.

The summer cattle season is all but over, and Marshal Wild Bill Hickok has kept the peace in Abilene, Kansas—not an easy job. The last marshal, legendary Thomas J. Smith, was killed in the line of duty.

Hickok is not popular with the Texans, having cleaned out the brothels the month before, on the order of the city council.

About 50 cowboys want to attend the city's Dickinson County Fair. When heavy rain sullies that venue, the boys wander from saloon to saloon on the main drag, bullying and intimidating patrons into buying them drinks. Some accounts suggest the cowboys pull this trick on Hickok, sweeping him off his feet and carrying him into the nearest saloon. Hickok humors the boys and buys them a round.

Rumors swirl that Texas gambler Phil Coe has sworn to get Hickok "before the frost." Many citizens make themselves scarce as the evening wears on, fearful that things may get out of hand.

At about 9 p.m., Hickok hears a shot fired outside the Alamo Saloon. He earlier warned the cowboys against carrying firearms, so he confronts the group standing in front of the Alamo and encounters Phil Coe, with a pistol in his hand. Coe claims he fired at a stray dog, but as he says this, he pulls another pistol and fires twice, one ball going through Hickok's coat and the other thudding into the ground between his legs. Hickok reacts in a flash and "as quick as thought," according to the *Chronicle*, pulls his two Colt Navy revolvers. He fires them, hitting Coe twice in the stomach.

Others in the crowd are hurt. When another man brandishing a pistol emerges from the shadows, Hickok, not recognizing him in the glare of the kerosene lamps and his nerves on high alert, instinctively fires. He kills Michael Williams, a personal friend of his and a one-time city jailer.

Hickok carries Williams into the Alamo, and lays him down on a billiard table, then turns and disarms everyone he can find. The marshal warns them all to clear out of town. Within an hour, the place is deserted.

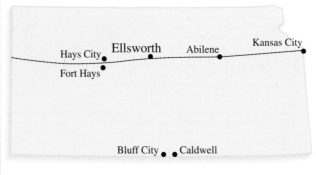

A street scene in Abilene, circa 1890s, with a medicine show drumming up business. The town is starting to look a little peaked—notice the sagging awning across the street.

Abilene: The First Queen of the Cowtowns

Named after the Biblical city of the plains, Abilene is the very first Kansas cowtown. Before Joseph McCoy set up operations here, it was just a small stop on the tracks of the Union Pacific Railway (Eastern Division) and a stagecoach stop prior to that. McCoy was a cattle buyer from Illinois who was anxious to find a shipping point clear of the restrictions against longhorn cattle. The Lone Star bovines carried a tic that transferred splenic fever (known as Texas fever). McCoy needed a shipping point far enough west so the incoming herds would not contaminate domestic stock. He found it at Abilene (of

course, as soon as farmers started moving in, the shipping point had to move). The first cattle season began on September 5, 1867, when the first train loaded with Texas cattle headed east. The season traditionally ran from May to October.

For the first three years, Abilene didn't even have a local lawman, until the appointment of Tom Smith in 1870. But he was murdered in November 1870. After a few stopgap policemen came and went, Wild Bill Hickok was appointed on April 15, 1871. He served eight months.

Aftermath: Odds & Ends

Wild Bill Hickok, "fired with marvelous rapidity and characteristic accuracy," *The Junction City Union* reported. However accurate he may have been, Hickok was profoundly affected by the shooting of his friend. In fact, he never fought with pistols again.

⸺ ☆ ⸺

As usual, in the aftermath of a Western gunfight, the participants are either eulogized or demonized, depending on which side is doing the telling. In the case of Hickok and Coe, they got the full spectrum of attributes: Coe was either "a red mouthed, bawling 'thug plug' Ugly … dangerous beast" or "a kind and generous hearted man well thought of by all who knew him." Conversely, in Texas papers, Hickok is referred to as a "blood thirsty wretch."

⸺ ☆ ⸺

Recommended: *The West of Wild Bill Hickok* and *They Called Him Wild Bill* by Joseph G. Rosa, published by the University of Oklahoma Press.

Wild Bill's remorse.

Abilene, as it looked while Hickok resided there. The 1871 cattle season ended with drovers facing financial losses. Some pushed their herds on to Waterville, while others held their cattle in Abilene. They hoped for higher prices, but a shortage of freight cars kept the prices low, leaving the drovers with little choice but to sell short or winter them. Either way, many cow men were in a sour mood.

ZIP ZAPPED!

ZIP WYATT VS EVERYONE IN WESTERN OKLAHOMA

ONE AGAINST 1,000

125 DAYS OF FIGHT AND FLIGHT

Zip Wyatt (at right) returns fire at the Hildreth posse as Ike Black is shot in the head.

Near Cainville, Oklahoma, Marion Hildreth and five other lawmen surround a cabin. After eating supper, Ike Black and Dick Yeager (a.k.a. Zip Wyatt) exit the cabin, arguing over a last chaw of tobacco. Deputy Hildreth shouts, "Throw up your hands!" The outlaws do, "but each hand contains a Winchester or Colt's revolver." Hildreth shoots Black in the head, killing him instantly.

While the posse shoots at Wyatt, the outlaw fires his Winchester "as fast as he [can] lever and pull the trigger," an eye-witness later says. A bullet strikes Wyatt close to the "nipple of the right breast … plowing a bad furrow half way around his body." Wyatt drops his Winchester but quickly retrieves it. He then shouts, "Marion Hildreth, you have killed the best man in Oklahoma!" before sprinting into a cornfield.

Seriously wounded, Wyatt tramples a path through the tall stalks, while the posse sends "rifle balls after him as rapidly as possible." Running east over a sand hill, Wyatt is in plain view for nearly a half mile. No one follows, however, because of the posse's "respect for his demonstration."

Two miles away, Wyatt encounters the young Dr. Edington. The doctor bluntly tells him, "You are not able to travel with that wound." Yet Wyatt replies, "I have to travel. Fix me up." After being treated, Wyatt commandeers the doctor's little buckskin horse and heads east.

Wyatt's wound is so bad that he can't ride anymore. He persuades a farmer in a lumber wagon to haul him to the Cimarron River. While wading across the river, he spots a 14-year-old boy driving a one-horse cart. Wyatt demands a ride. "Frightened nearly out of his senses," the boy drives

> **"Marion Hildreth, you have killed the best man in Oklahoma!"**
> –*Zip Wyatt*

Wyatt "at top speed 25 miles east into southwestern Garfield County." He releases the boy and drives on in the cart.

The next day, a 40-man posse tracks Wyatt to Turkey Creek and then detours into Hennessey to get fresh mounts. At 2 p.m., the posse learns that Wyatt has crossed the Rock Island Railroad tracks about five miles south of Enid. At Waukomis, the lawmen telegraph the Garfield County sheriff for assistance. In Skeleton Creek Valley, 14 miles to the east, the posse discovers an abandoned cart and horse. They have no idea how close they are to the outlaw.

At Skeleton Creek, Wyatt stops by a cabin, demanding food and a horse. John Daily notes the dry blood on the front of the outlaw's brown shirt and his three weeks' growth of beard. Daily tells Wyatt he can't help him. Stumbling on, Wyatt finally finds a horse; when that one tires, he finds another and then another.

By August 4, multiple posses have dogged Wyatt's trail southeast of Sheridan. Five miles south of Marshall, Wyatt's last horse is found grazing. The fugitive's tracks lead to a cornfield on Alvin Ross' farm. An exhausted Wyatt lies there, on a sandy mound where the corn won't grow.

The posse surrounds the field, while three volunteers wade in (one eventually turns back). They track Wyatt's faltering footprints through the corn rows until they discover the sleeping outlaw, lying with his Winchester in his right hand and a cedar-handled Colt revolver near the other.

Leveling their Winchesters, the two men call out: "Up with your hands Dick—we've got you!"

Wyatt's eyes pop open, and he instinctively grabs his weapons. Both posse members fire simultaneously, "the balls taking effect two inches apart in the outlaw's right hip and abdomen."

After being tracked by 1,000 men and eluding capture for 125 days, Zip Wyatt lies mortally wounded. His long flight and fight are finally over.

Events Leading Up to the Gunfight on August 2, 1895

June 4

After numerous robberies, the Wyatt-Black Gang (also called the Zip Wyatt Gang) is hiding in its Gyp Hills cave (see below) when the members are attacked by a posse led by Sheriff Clay McGrath. The fight is "kept up one whole day," and the lawmen kill one horse and capture half the gang: Belle Black and Jennie Freeman. The female outlaws report that their men have been wounded—Wyatt has been shot through the left arm, and Ike Black in the right heel—but, in spite of their wounds, the men escape on foot.

July 19

Freeman's father tells a neighbor (who alerts authorities) that Wyatt and Black were at his house near Sheridan while he was away, and that he is "afraid of them" and expects them back in a day or two.

July 25

Posing as lawmen, two riders believed to be Wyatt and Black take supper at a farm near Winnview and make "suave inquires" as to the best place to buy supplies. They ride a few miles to Oxley and rob the general store and post office.

Heading back to their hideout in the Gyp Hills, they find themselves surrounded in camp at the head of Salt Creek. In the ensuing gunfight, a Blaine County deputy sheriff is wounded in the left shoulder, but the outlaws escape, once again, on foot.

Late in the evening, the two come out of the hills, five miles west of Okeene, steal a horse and cart from a farmer, and slip through picket lines, with Wyatt "playing a French harp." (Wyatt evidently put the guards at ease by calmly playing his mouth organ.)

July 29

A nine-man posse from Lacey trails the outlaws to the Gyp Hills and follows the two five miles farther to a canyon.

The posse again surrounds the outlaws. A running gunfight ensues and lasts about 25 minutes; "the outlaws [are] firing faster than we," says Jack Ward, one of the posse members. Ward later reports the two "passed out of the canyon near me, and fired at me. I fired deliberately at [Wyatt] three times ... felt sure I struck him once in the breast ... he fell twice." The success is short-lived. The outlaws capture two of the posse members' horses and, once again, they escape.

July 31

The outlaws take a "zig-zagging course" along the North Canadian River, with several posses (reported to be 200 members strong) in hot pursuit.

Prime Bandit Country

In this remote part of the Oklahoma Territory, the Gyp Hills (left), also called the Glass Mountains because of the way the steep red slopes glisten in the sun, rise abruptly from the plains of Northern Blaine and Southern Woods (now Major) Counties. This region is the rendezvous point for the Wyatt-Black Gang.

– All Photos True West Archives unless otherwise noted –

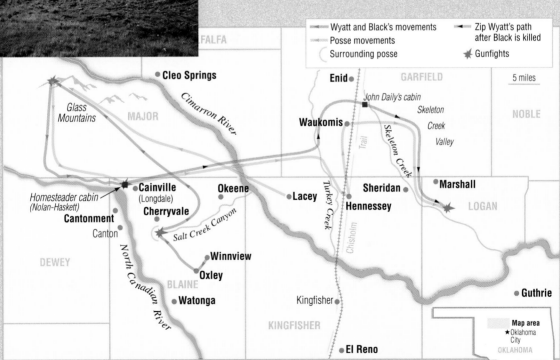

Following his escape from the federal jail in Guthrie in 1891, Wyatt makes his way up the Cimarron River into Southern Woods County. Using the alias Dick Yeager, he finds refuge with Matt Freeman (husband of Jennie), at his claim above the river south of Cleo Springs. Wyatt's partner, Ike Black, a former policeman in El Reno and now a fugitive, homesteads southwest of Watonga. They choose as their hideout a cave near the head of Salt Creek Canyon, 10 miles north of Watonga and south of Cherryvale (present-day Southard)—a hideout also used by the Dalton Gang. The drifting sands of the Salt Plain make "it almost impossible for a posse to follow."

Cheyennes Outsmart Zip

Nathaniel Ellsworth Wyatt (inset), a.k.a. Zip Wyatt, alias Dick Yeager. As a cowboy in the Cherokee Outlet, he is said to be a good horseman, expert shot and fond of cheap whiskey. Yet he can be bested. On a bluff on the west side of the North Canadian River, roughly midway between Fort Reno and Fort Supply, lays Cantonment (above), an abandoned military camp. The stone buildings serve as a sub-agency for the Cheyenne and Arapaho tribes, which graze many unattended horses on the unfenced prairie. When the Wyatt-Black Gang steal a small herd from there to drive into Kansas and sell to crooked buyers, Cheyenne Chief Henry Roman Nose and his braves intercept the gang and drive the herd back into the Gyp Hills.

"Move, or I'll put some smoke between your eyes."

–Zip Wyatt, to a slow-moving homesteader

Belle Black (at left) and Jennie Freeman ride with the outlaws until they are captured on June 4, 1895. No known photos of the two have surfaced.

Female Half of Wyatt-Black Gang

"The [Belle] Black woman is small, heavy set, with dark hair and blue eyes; the Freeman woman [Pearl or Jennie] is rather tall, very slim build, of light complexion, and has her hair shingled close."

—Oklahoma State Capital

"Mrs. [Jennie] Freeman is small of stature and quite handsome and when dressed in male attire is the very picture of a boy in his teens. She wears her hair short and it curls around the bill of her cap."

—The Wichita Eagle

Ike Black's body is left where he fell until a local justice of the peace can be summoned. Nothing is found on his person but a "photograph of the woman who has been his mistress, and $1.50 in money." The body is taken to Alva, where it is photographed (above) and buried at county expense.

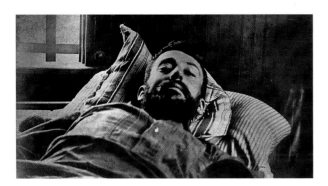

Zip Wyatt in the Garfield County jail, wounded and dying, following his capture near Sheridan.

A Legendary Lawman on Wyatt's Trail

"Zip Wyatt has been pursued by myself and other deputies for several months. On the 3rd inst. he was reported near Enid, and I went there, and took up his trail, but did not arrest him, as a party of farmers, who were also pursuing him, had already secured him before I could overtake him. As he was so badly wounded as to be considered incurable, and may die at any moment, I recommend that such testimony as may establish his identity be taken at once in the jail where he is now confined. (Enid) This, that it may be positively known that he, who is wanted for many crimes, is no longer at large, and that if no other complaints are entered against him, he be held on this."

—*(Signed) C. Madsen, Dep. USM.*

U.S. Deputy Marshal Chris Madsen, c. 1937, emigrated to the U.S. from Denmark around 1870 and joined the army, eventually becoming a federal deputy in the 1890s for the Western Oklahoma Territory.

– COURTESY WESTERN HISTORY COLLECTIONS, UNIVERSITY OF OKLAHOMA LIBRARY –

Aftermath: Odds & Ends

After being shot on August 4, Zip Wyatt was moved to a small church in Sheridan, where numerous posses from various jurisdictions fought over the prisoner and the reward. The half-conscious Wyatt listened to the dispute for some time, until finally whispering to a deputy: "If you'll give me my six-shooter for about two seconds, I'll stop the argument."

A "distinguished guest" at the Garfield County jail, Wyatt lived in pain and "a bunch of suffering humanity," as one of the newspapers put it, until 6:30 p.m. on September 6. Before Wyatt's death, a doctor asked him, "This is your last day on earth. Is there anyone you wish to see or anything you wish to say?" A grinning Wyatt replied, "Nobody to see, Doc, an' nothin' to say."

A grand jury discharged Belle Black and Jennie Freeman, finding "no evidence of a criminal nature against them, other than their presence with the two outlaws." Freeman, according to an 1898 Oklahoma newspaper, "was converted during the year she spent in the federal jail, and is now travelling as an evangelist." Black apparently settled down with a new husband and raised a family, successfully hiding her outlaw past.

Recommended: *Desperado from Cowboy Flat: The Saga of "Zip" Wyatt* by Glenn Shirley, published by Barbed Wire Press.

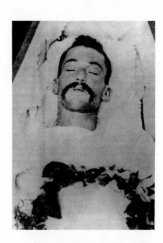

No relative would claim Wyatt's remains, so he was buried in a pauper's field at Garfield County's expense. The funeral was attended only by local carpenter Dan C. Bass, who fashioned Wyatt's pine coffin, the grave digger and the jail pup, who Wyatt befriended during his incarceration.

HELL'S IN SESSION

CALDWELL LAWMEN VS TEXAS COWBOYS

"Hide out little ones!"

DECEMBER 17, 1881

Cowboy James Talbot gets word that his Texas pards are in a jam—again. Hitching a ride on a passing wagon, he and former Deputy Marshal Dan Jones, a.k.a. Red Bill, make their way to the heart of the trouble.

Driver Newt Miller reins up the wagon at the intersection of Fifth and Main Streets in downtown Caldwell, Kansas. A crowd of about 30 has gathered around the foot of the stairs leading to the police court, where City Marshal John Wilson and Deputy Bill Fossett are escorting Texas cowboys Jim Martin and Bob Munson (arrested for rowdy behavior, carrying firearms and making threats). Talbot steps off the wagon and says, "Hold on there boys. Hold on."

Talbot asks the prisoners where they are being taken and why, then boldly remarks that they don't have to pay a fine "if they don't want to."

Sensing trouble, Marshal Wilson pulls out two six-shooters, but Martin and Munson take advantage of the surging crowd as they duck behind bystanders and dodge their way clear.

Someone hands Talbot a pistol (one report states two), and he fires off several rounds to scatter the crowd, saying as he does, "Hide out little ones!" As the heavily outnumbered lawmen run for cover, shots are heard coming from South Main Street, in the area of Mike Meagher's saloon. Talbot and his cowboys move south, shooting out the window panes as they run along the street. Emptying his pistol, Talbot cries, "Boys, come to my house, get your Winchesters and give them hell." The cowboys follow Talbot to his house for the weapons, while citizens arm themselves at the local mercantiles on Main.

Re-armed with long rifles, the cowboys spread out and take different routes back into the action. Talbot takes up a position at a small storage shed in the alley behind the Pulaski Building. Talbot aims at ex-mayor Mike Meagher, who is about 65 feet away from the shed. Meagher spots him and ducks the shot, which rakes the bricks and sends mortar flying. The two duel it out at their respective corners for some time.

Seeking an advantage, Meagher backtracks to Main and runs to the south side of the Pulaski Building, traversing the wall to hopefully flank Talbot. Meanwhile, Talbot has worked his way north from the shed and stands exposed on the sidewalk on the south side of Fifth Street. As Meagher and two others clear the corner, Talbot sees his rival first, raises his Winchester and fires, the bullet striking Meagher in the chest. Meagher sinks to the ground, telling Ed Rathburn, who stands next to him, "Tell my wife I have got it at last." Taken into Sherer's barbershop on Main, Meagher dies within a half hour.

Talbot retreats toward his house, zig-zagging, running and rolling, as numerous balls kick up the dust all around him. Talbot joins several of the cowboys at his home, where they reconnoiter and make plans for an escape. Talbot sends a friend out to saddle his horse.

Looking out the back of his store on Main, ex-mayor H.N. Hubble notices the cowboys' horses being saddled in the common area east of the Red Light Saloon. Grabbing his Winchester, Hubble exits his store, crosses the alley and takes up a position in front of "Lengthy" Jones' blacksmith shop, from where he opens fire on the cowboys' horses, killing several. Also fatally hit by gunfire is the manager of the Red Light, George Speer (who was saddling Talbot's horse); cowboy Doug Hill is shot in the heel.

During a half-hour lull, four of the cowboys make a raid on George Kalbfleisch's Livery stable. At gunpoint, they demand four saddled horses. The cowboys leave with the horses and an extra saddle for good measure. Soon after, cowboy Dick Eddleman enters the stable, brandishing a revolver and ordering the livery men to saddle a horse for him. Incredibly, they refuse. Eddleman sheepishly puts up his pistol, asks that they "not give him away" and slinks off.

Five cowboys, Jim Talbot, Bob Bigtree, Bob Munson, Jim Martin and Doug Hill, ride east out of town. The fight is over, but a party of citizens takes up pursuit and the chase is on.

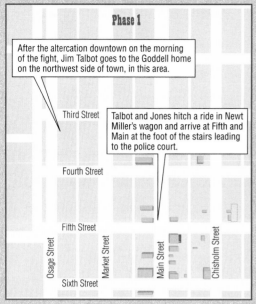

Phase 1

After the altercation downtown on the morning of the fight, Jim Talbot goes to the Goddell home on the northwest side of town, in this area.

Talbot and Jones hitch a ride in Newt Miller's wagon and arrive at Fifth and Main at the foot of the stairs leading to the police court.

Third Street

Fourth Street

Fifth Street

Sixth Street

Osage Street
Market Street
Main Street
Chisholm Street

> "Talbot always had quite a following among the cowboys and many of them made his home their headquarters when visiting the town."
>
> —*Wellington Monitor Press*

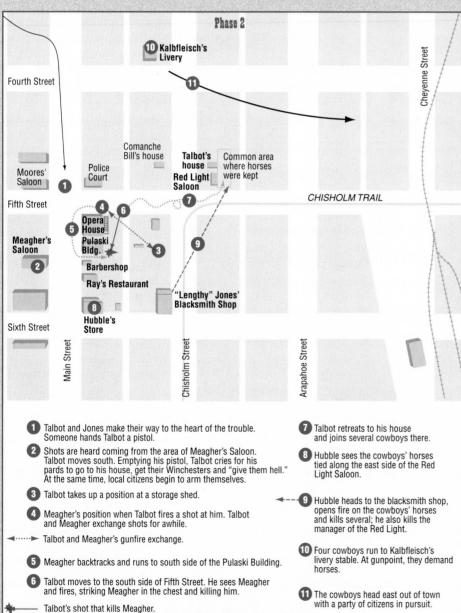

Phase 2

10 Kalbfleisch's Livery

11

Fourth Street

Cheyenne Street

Moores' Saloon
1

Police Court

Comanche Bill's house

Talbot's house
Red Light Saloon

Common area where horses were kept

CHISHOLM TRAIL

Fifth Street

4 **6**
Opera House
5 **Pulaski Bldg.**
3
9
7

Meagher's Saloon
2

Barbershop

Ray's Restaurant

"Lengthy" Jones' Blacksmith Shop

8
Hubble's Store

Sixth Street

Main Street
Chisholm Street
Arapahoe Street

1 Talbot and Jones make their way to the heart of the trouble. Someone hands Talbot a pistol.

2 Shots are heard coming from the area of Meagher's Saloon. Talbot moves south. Emptying his pistol, Talbot cries for his pards to go to his house, get their Winchesters and "give them hell." At the same time, local citizens begin to arm themselves.

3 Talbot takes up a position at a storage shed.

4 Meagher's position when Talbot fires a shot at him. Talbot and Meagher exchange shots for awhile.

← → Talbot and Meagher's gunfire exchange.

5 Meagher backtracks and runs to south side of the Pulaski Building.

6 Talbot moves to the south side of Fifth Street. He sees Meagher and fires, striking Meagher in the chest and killing him.

← Talbot's shot that kills Meagher.

7 Talbot retreats to his house and joins several cowboys there.

8 Hubble sees the cowboys' horses tied along the east side of the Red Light Saloon.

9 Hubble heads to the blacksmith shop, opens fire on the cowboys' horses and kills several; he also kills the manager of the Red Light.

10 Four cowboys run to Kalbfleisch's livery stable. At gunpoint, they demand horses.

11 The cowboys head east out of town with a party of citizens in pursuit.

The Backstory

The night before the shoot-out, a group of cowboys, led by Jim Talbot and attended by their prostitutes, hoot and holler, yelling obscenities at a Friday-night presentation of the play "Uncle Tom's Cabin" in the Opera House. The editor of the local paper requests their leader, Talbot, "desist from his obscenity," but the cowboy calls him out and "declares that he would 'fix him the next day.'"

The next morning, Mike Meagher and City Marshal John Wilson go to Ren Moores' saloon to arrest cowboy Tom Love for firing a revolver in the building (he allegedly shot out a window). With Love are Comanche Bill Mankin, Bob Munson and Dick Eddleman, who are armed with "revolvers, needle guns and Winchesters," as an eyewitness later testifies.

Wilson and Meagher head to the jail with Love, but the two are overtaken by Talbot and his cowboy pards at the intersection of Main and Fifth. Meagher, who is unarmed, tells them, "You fellows won't shoot," as he backs up the Opera House stairs. Wilson aims his weapon at the cowboys and threatens to shoot the first one who makes a move.

Even though the cowboys are still under arrest, they are allowed to return to Ray's Restaurant to finish their breakfast. They continue making threats against Meagher and the officers for what they feel is unfair harassment.

At some point in the late morning, Talbot leaves the cowboys and, taking his wife and children, goes to the Goddell home (see map, top left) and eats supper (noonday meal) before a friend comes and warns him the Boys are in trouble again. It's interesting to note that Talbot appears to be sober and unarmed at the time. The same can't be said for the other cowboys in the melee, or some of the lawmen. Eyewitnesses will later claim that both Wilson and Meagher were drunk at the time of the afternoon shoot-out.

A Caldwell home, c. 1880s.

— COURTESY LEN GRATTERI —

Meagher Motives

Mike Meagher had been the city marshal in Wichita and was efficient (he served five terms with only one killing by his hand). Wyatt Earp even served as one of his deputies.

After he moved to Caldwell, Meagher (pronounced mâr—like mayor) was offered the position of marshal, but he repeatedly turned it down (during an emergency, he will serve as the city's marshal for five days in 1881). Instead, he aspired to be mayor, for which he was elected in April 1880 (which would make him "Mayor Mayor").

During his term, he discharged City Marshal George Flatt because he disapproved of Flatt's confrontational way of law enforcement. On June 18, 1880, a drunken Flatt toured Caldwell's saloons, voicing his complaints about Meagher and the police. Shortly after midnight, he was fatally shot in the street. Meagher and his appointed lawmen became suspects in the killing but, ultimately, were discharged of the crime.

After Talbot killed Meagher in the December 17, 1881, shoot-out, some local conspiracy theorists believed that Talbot had killed Meagher to avenge Flatt's murder (Talbot's wife was allegedly related to Flatt).

Other locals felt the motive was much simpler, recalling an altercation between Talbot and Meagher two weeks before the shoot-out (no contemporary reports confirm the run-in). Talbot had been racing his horse on the streets of Caldwell when Meagher and police officer John Wilson stopped him for "fast driving." Talbot drew his revolver, which he used to strike each of the lawmen across the hands, breaking their hold on his bridle and allowing him to ride away.

Other rumors attributed to the riff included a tale that Talbot and five of his crew had called for drinks "'for the crowd" in Meagher's Arcade Saloon, then refused to pay, hoping to "draw Mike into a quarrel." "Comanche Bill took a pistol away from [cowboy Tom] Love who was trying to shoot Meagher in his saloon," reported eyewitness Edward Heiflingler.

Author Robert DeArment pins the motive on Meagher's only kill. When Meagher was serving his fifth term as Wichita city marshal, Sylvester Powell fired three shots at Meagher from an alleyway, then ran. Meagher caught up to him and fired one shot, killing the young stage driver on New Year's Day 1877. So, what's the connection? DeArment says Powell was Talbot's favorite cousin.

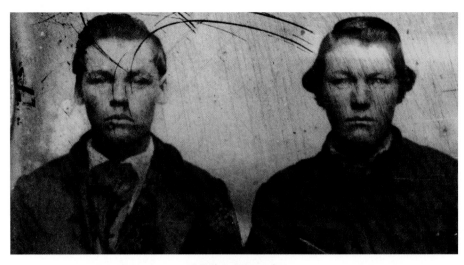

A Twin's Revenge?

The Meagher twins, John (left) and Mike, were born in County Queens, Ireland, on April 4, 1843. Following the great Irish potato famines in 1845-46, the family emigrated to the U.S., settling first in New York state and later Illinois before the boys set out for the frontier and Kansas. Some believe John avenged his brother's death some 15 years after the Talbot shooting.

The Cowboys

Most of Talbot's men came up the Chisholm Trail from Texas to Caldwell, Kansas, with a herd of cattle. One cowboy said of Talbot, "He was a real cowman if I ever saw one, but so damn tough he could hardly sleep with himself."

James Talbot: (Real name James Sherman), about five feet, 10 inches high; weight about 170 pounds; light complexion; light-colored mustache and whiskers; light blue or gray eyes; broad face; high cheek bones; nose turned up a little at end. Another description of him: "smooth faced and destitute of anything approaching a smile, with a course, rough voice and a cold, dead looking grey eye."

Doug Hill: (Real name Bob Johnson), medium size; slim build; hump shouldered; blue eyes; blondish hair and mustache; disfigured left hand, missing pinky, from fight with a Mexican vaquero at a Millet ranch line camp.

Bob Munson: Blue eyes; sandy hair and mustache; wanted for murder in Eastland County, Texas.

Jim Martin: Average height; heavy build; light complexion; light blue eyes; face, round and clean shaven; thumbnail shot off on right hand.

Bob Bigtree: Six feet in height; weight about 150 pounds; his "coarse" features are clean shaven; he has "stoop shoulders and hollow breast."

Tom Love: (Real name Thomas Love Culbreth), no description of him is known to exist; wanted for murder in Milam County, Texas, and has a reward of $200 on his head.

A Dangerous Crew

No known photos exist of the Caldwell cowboys. Here are illustrations based on their descriptions. From left: Doug Hill (note mangled hand), Jim Talbot, Bob Munson, Jim Martin, Bob Bigtree and Tom Love (upper right).

> "The bold and fearless form of Jim Talbot was the center of the firing. He stood bravely to the front, with revolver in each hand, firing at the men he premeditated to kill."
>
> —*A cowboy partisan, who heard about the fight from Talbot's friends weeks later*

Fight started here at Fifth and Main.

Police station on second floor.

Downtown Caldwell (top), c. 1885. We're looking north on Main from below Sixth Street. In the bottom photo we are looking east on Fifth from Market towards the origin of the fight.

– COURTESY LEN GRATTERI –

The Cowboy's Caldwell: The Wildest of the Wild

Hoping to capitalize on the Texas cattle trade, Wichita residents founded Caldwell in March 1871, planting it 80 miles south of their hometown and right on the Kansas-Oklahoma line (the border originally dissected the town, until a correction moved it south a few miles).

In 1879, the Atchison, Topeka and Santa Fe Railroad announced it would build a spur line south from Wichita to the border town. Seeing a golden opportunity, veteran Wichita lawman Mike Meagher moved with his wife to Caldwell and opened the Arcade Saloon with a partner.

Caldwell quickly became the wildest of all the Kansas cowtowns, amassing more killings and blowing through more lawmen—Caldwell had 14 different city marshals in a five-year period, with half of them dying—than Wichita, Ellsworth or Dodge City.

Aftermath: Odds & Ends

After a wild chase, the five cowboys abandoned their horses and holed up in a canyon about 12 miles from Caldwell. Surrounded by posse members, a fight was kept up until dark with several wounded on both sides. Reinforcements from Caldwell and surrounding areas arrived at about 10 p.m., but during the night, the outlaws escaped on foot.

☆

John Wilson was shot to death in Wellington, Kansas, in December 1884. Several of the participants in the Caldwell shoot-out became lawmen, including cowboy Tom Love (also a successful rancher), who helped track down outlaw Bill Cook, a.k.a., Cherokee Kid.

☆

Thirteen years after the shoot-out, an unknown informer squealed on the whereabouts of James Talbot, who was then under arrest in northern California and going by his real name, J.D. Sherman. Kansas authorities brought Talbot back to Kansas, where he was tried twice for the murder of Mike Meagher. On April 8, 1895, a hung jury set Talbot free (an attorney remarked: "We started out to hang one man and hung twelve instead"). In September, a jury found him not guilty. Sherman went home to Ukiah, California, and was involved in several other odd skirmishes (a range war and his wife leaving him for another cowboy). He was shot dead on the evening of August 11, 1896, while riding a mule with a sack of flour in front of him on the saddle. Some suspected the cowboy who had hooked up with Sherman's wife, while others suspected Mike Meagher's twin brother, John, who had vowed revenge for some time. The case has never been solved.

☆

Recommended: *George and Maggie and the Red Light Saloon* by Rod Cook, published by iUniverse; *Revenge! And Other True Tales of the Old West* by Robert K. DeArment, published by Scarlet Mask.

ONE HELL-FIRIN' MINUTE OF SMOKIN' ACTION

DEPUTY ED SHORT VS BLACK-FACED CHARLEY BRYANT

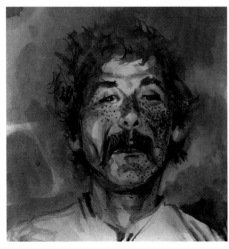

Charley got his nickname from a black powder explosion that hit his face.

AUGUST 22, 1891

Deputy Ed Short has learned that the ill man lodging at the Rock Island Railroad hotel in Hennessey, Oklahoma, is none other than "Black-Faced" Charley Bryant, an extremely dangerous member of the Dalton outlaw gang currently terrorizing the territory.

Surprising Bryant in his room, Short clamps cuffs on him. His only problem: the closest secure jail is about 140 miles away in Wichita, Kansas.

The next day, Short, wearing two six-shooters and carrying a Winchester rifle, marches his prisoner to the train depot. Conductor Jim Collins allows Short to ride with his prisoner in the mail and baggage car, away from the other passengers. As they board, Bryant complains that his arms ache (his hands are manacled behind his back). Short relents and uncuffs his prisoner's hands, recuffing Bryant's hands in front of him. The train chugs away from the station; a postal agent is their only companion.

As the train slows for its first stop, in Waukomis, Short spots several horsemen approaching at a gallop. Concerned that a rescue attempt is under way, Short hands the postal agent one of his revolvers and tells him to watch Bryant. The deputy steps onto the platform, rifle in hand, to check out the suspicious-looking riders. The agent, busy sorting mail to be dropped at Waukomis, sticks the pistol in one of the letter pigeonholes and concentrates on his job.

Bryant seizes the opportunity. In a flash, he snatches up the six-shooter with his manacled hands. He heads out on the platform to confront Short and make his escape.

Short quickly brings up his Winchester and covers Bryant. For a brief second, officer and outlaw glare at each other over leveled weapons. Both open fire at point-blank range; Bryant cocks the hammer and triggers the Colt revolver, and Short levers and fires his Winchester.

Deputy Ed Short escorts dangerous fugitive Charley Bryant across the train platform in Hennessey, Oklahoma. Short makes one mistake on this prisoner transfer, and it will be fatal.

> "I got my man, but he got me, too."
>
> –Ed Short

Struck in the heart and spinal cord, Bryant falls, gasping his last breath. Although mortally wounded himself, Short drops his rifle and grasps the legs of the outlaw, yelling for help. Conductor Collins rushes to his assistance.

Together, they pull Bryant's body back onto the platform.

As more help arrives, Short collapses. Stretched out on the platform beside Bryant's body, Short, just before he dies, says, "I got my man, but he got me, too. I would like to see my mother."

As for Bryant, he got his wish.

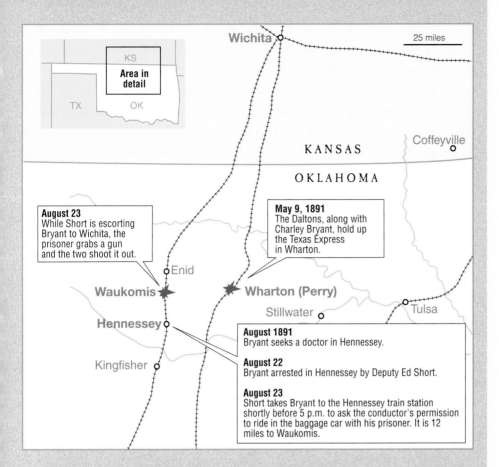

Wichita

25 miles

KS
Area in detail

TX   OK

KANSAS

OKLAHOMA

Coffeyville

May 9, 1891
The Daltons, along with Charley Bryant, hold up the Texas Express in Wharton.

August 23
While Short is escorting Bryant to Wichita, the prisoner grabs a gun and the two shoot it out.

Enid

Waukomis

Wharton (Perry)

Hennessey

Stillwater

Tulsa

Kingfisher

August 1891
Bryant seeks a doctor in Hennessey.

August 22
Bryant arrested in Hennessey by Deputy Ed Short.

August 23
Short takes Bryant to the Hennessey train station shortly before 5 p.m. to ask the conductor's permission to ride in the baggage car with his prisoner. It is 12 miles to Waukomis.

A Fearless Lawman's Tragic End

Born and raised in Indiana, Ed Short, 17, headed west to Kansas to become a cowboy. He worked cattle around Hunnewell and Caldwell, and may have worked in law enforcement before moving to Stevens County.

Descriptions of Short vary. Glenn Shirley called him "small of stature, quiet in manner, and dudish in dress … not a man to inspire fear. He was a bad man in the sense that he was fearless. Like the dime-novel hero, he reveled in deeds of blood and valor, but there was little bravado about him." Sam Riding, an old-timer who claimed to know Short, said he was "of large and robust physique and commanding appearance. He had the appearance of a fearless and effective officer, which he was." Both writers agreed that Short was blond.

We know that Short was actively involved in Kansas' county seat wars. He served as a lawman in Woodsdale; the citizens appreciated his work so much that they presented him with a specially engraved Colt—which he later lost in a fight with representatives of a rival town. He married in 1887, but his wife committed suicide after just five months into wedlock.

Short joined the land rush in 1889 and settled in Hennessey in the Indian Territory, where he was elected city

marshal in that town's first municipal election. When Oklahoma Territory was established in 1890, U.S. Marshal William Grimes appointed him one of his first deputies.

The next year, Charley Bryant got his wish to die in "one hell-firin' minute of smokin' action." Short (below, at top) was laid out next to the dead outlaw, where he too expired. It's a sad note that Short lost his life for being compassionate. Had Bryant's hands been kept manacled behind him, he likely could not have orchestrated the bloody finale.

Aftermath: Odds & Ends

The mother Ed Short never got to see again, Mrs. L.M. Short of Osgood, Indiana, was presented with a check for $500, donated by the Santa Fe Railroad. The reward had been offered by the railway line for the arrest and conviction of any member of the Dalton gang who had held up a Santa Fe train in Wharton, Indian Territory, on May 9, 1891.

⸺ ☆ ⸺

It's unclear what illness "Black-Faced" Charley Bryant suffered from in Hennessey. Some accounts state it was malaria. Others posit that he was being treated for a venereal disease. It's also not clear how old the Texas native was when he died.

Black-Faced Charley Bryant

⸺ ☆ ⸺

Short was buried in Osgood. Bryant's body was claimed by relatives and transported to Decatur, Texas. His body is probably buried in the cemetery there, along with several of his kin, but no tombstone marks his grave.

⸺ ☆ ⸺

Recommended: *Ballots and Bullets: The Bloody County Seat Wars of Kansas* by Robert DeArment, published by University of Oklahoma Press; and *Deadly Affrays* by Robert Ernst, published by Scarlet Mask.

FOREWARNED & FOREARMED

BEN THOMPSON & KING FISHER VS JOE FOSTER & BILLY SIMMS

Death waits behind the curtain.

Fresh off the train from Austin, Texas, newly minted drinking pards, Ben Thompson and acting Uvalde County Sheriff John King Fisher, take in the sights and sounds of San Antonio.

The dynamic drinking duo make their first stop at Turner Hall Opera House (see map, opposite page), where they take in a performance of "Lady Audley's Secret," starring Ada Gray. After the play, the two visit several saloons before a hack drops them off in front of the Vaudeville Theatre. Nearing 10 p.m., they stand outside, visiting, for about a half hour before they enter the Vaudeville.

Both men stop at the bar for a drink as co-owner Billy Simms (or Sims) and special policeman Jacob Coy stroll over and greet Thompson and Fisher. The four proceed upstairs to watch the show. Taking a seat in the dress circle, Thompson calls for another drink and Fisher orders a cigar.

Thompson starts making rude comments about his killing of Jack Harris, an event now two years old. But the tension rises when saloon co-owner Joe Foster joins the group. Thompson calls Foster a thief and the

Drinking heavily most of the day, Ben Thompson strikes a porter on the train. Blood has splattered on his silk hat, so Thompson cuts away the crown and sticks a knife in the brim. Wearing his new, bizarre headgear, he steps off the train with John King Fisher to take in the sights of San Antonio. Ben's brother Billy says Ben buys a new hat before arriving at the Vaudeville Theatre.

real target of his earlier shooting ("That is the son of a bitch I wanted to kill").

Fisher suggests they go downstairs to the bar, and all agree. As they reach the door leading to the stairs (see map), Thompson turns to shake Foster's hand, but the saloon proprietor refuses.

It is a Wednesday night at the Vaudeville, with the usual fare on stage, as Thompson and Fisher take a seat in the dress circle.

Thompson pulls a pistol and pistol whips Foster about the mouth (one version has him putting the barrel in Foster's mouth). Seeing this, Coy tries to grab the barrel of Thompson's pistol as a shot rings out.

All hell breaks loose as everyone reaches for their hardware and a thunderous volley of shots (some say 20) rips through the theater. Fisher and Thompson are hit multiple times, and Foster takes a bullet in the leg. As blood and gore welter in the doorway and on the stairs leading to the street, friends help Foster down the stairs to safety as his leg bleeds badly.

This is the official San Antonio version of the fight. An autopsy, performed on Thompson when his body is returned to Austin, will hint at a darker version of events.

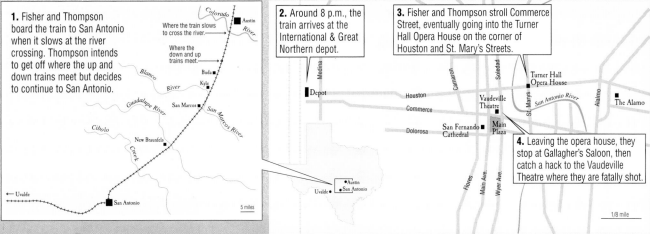

1. Fisher and Thompson board the train to San Antonio when it slows at the river crossing. Thompson intends to get off where the up and down trains meet but decides to continue to San Antonio.

2. Around 8 p.m., the train arrives at the International & Great Northern depot.

3. Fisher and Thompson stroll Commerce Street, eventually going into the Turner Hall Opera House on the corner of Houston and St. Mary's Streets.

4. Leaving the opera house, they stop at Gallagher's Saloon, then catch a hack to the Vaudeville Theatre where they are fatally shot.

The Vaudeville Theatre was first opened in 1872 by partners Jack Harris, Joe Foster and Billy Simms.

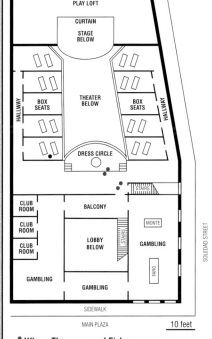

Upstairs Floorplan of the Vaudeville Theatre

PLAY LOFT
CURTAIN
STAGE BELOW
HALLWAY
BOX SEATS
THEATER BELOW
BOX SEATS
HALLWAY
DRESS CIRCLE
CLUB ROOM
BALCONY
STAIRS
CLUB ROOM
MONTE
CLUB ROOM
LOBBY BELOW
STAIRS
GAMBLING
FARO
GAMBLING
GAMBLING
SOLEDAD STREET
SIDEWALK
MAIN PLAZA   10 feet

• Where Thompson and Fisher are standing when shot.

• Location of Thompson and Fisher's bodies.

• Location of the shooters.

Sources: *Legendary Watering Holes: The Saloons that Made Texas Famous* and Tom Bicknell.

Billy Simms

King Fisher

Jack Harris

Ben Thompson

Deadliest Gunfighters Dealt a Deadly Hand

In 1884, Ben Thompson and King Fisher are two of the deadliest gunfighters on the loose in Texas, with one caveat: John Wesley Hardin is in prison at this time. Ironically, both Thompson and Fisher have led charmed lives (see time line, p. 100) until they meet in Austin and travel together to San Antonio. Wearing a hat, sans crown, with a knife stuck in it, Thompson must have looked quite bizarre, but not half as macabre as he and Fisher will look just outside the dress circle of the upstairs balcony at the Vaudeville Theatre (see diagram, above).

Texas Time line: What Goes Around, Comes Around

Ben Thompson and King Fisher share a charmed life, right up until the moment they meet.

Of the two shootists, the English-born Thompson gets the jump, having participated in three shooting scrapes by his 18th birthday. After a stint in the Confederate cavalry during the Civil War, Thompson is jailed, escapes, flees to Mexico and serves in Maximilian's army, rising to the rank of major.

Back in the U.S., Ben Thompson joins forces with Phil Coe and Tom Bowles in a saloon-gambling operation in Austin, Texas.

As we pick up their time line, both men begin their final arc by serving time in prison:

1868

After a dust-up with his brother-in-law, Thompson serves time in a Huntsville, Texas, prison, serving two years of a four-year sentence. He is released in 1870.

October 1870

Sentenced to two years in a Huntsville prison for "housebreaking," John King Fisher serves four months before he is given a pardon.

October 5, 1871

Wild Bill Hickok kills Thompson's partner Phil Coe in front of the Alamo Saloon in Abilene, Kansas (see p. 86). After a buggy accident injures his wife, Thompson and his family return to Austin, Texas.

June 4, 1876

Texas Rangers capture Fisher and nine of his gang, but the prisoners are released due to lack of evidence.

December 25, 1876

In Austin, Thompson fatally shoots theatre owner Mark Wilson and wounds bartender Charles Mathews. He is arrested but ultimately acquitted.

May 16, 1877

On charges of murder and horse stealing, Fisher is again arrested by Texas Rangers.

November 19, 1877

Fisher is imprisoned in the "Bat Cave" jail in San Antonio for five months until released on $25,000 bond (put up by prominent ranchers). While held in the jail, Fisher is sent daily restaurant meals by local saloon owner Joe Foster, and at Foster's expense.

May 13, 1878

Fisher has 15 indictments pending against him, but the "indictments" mysteriously turn up missing. Fisher makes bond in six of the cases, with help from the same seven ranchers.

1879

In Colorado, Thompson enlists on the side of the Santa Fe Railway in its bloodless war with the Denver & Rio Grande, earning a $5,000 fee.

December 1880

Thompson is elected city marshal of Austin. Crime is reported at an all-time low, and he is re-elected to the post in 1881.

April 21, 1881

Fisher is found not guilty on charges of murdering two Mexicans, and, in May, he is acquitted or dismissed on all other charges brought against him. Fisher makes a vow that he will never be charged with any offense again.

July 11, 1882

On a bender, Thompson fatally shoots Jack Harris, owner of the Vaudeville Theatre in San Antonio. He is acquitted of the crime but resigns his post as city marshal.

Early 1883

At the request of Sheriff Boatright, Fisher becomes a deputy sheriff of Uvalde County. In October, when an indictment is returned against the sheriff, Fisher becomes acting sheriff.

March 10, 1884

Fisher travels by rail to the Texas capital to learn more about a new state statute that makes fence cutting a felony. He meets Thompson here for the first time, and the two hit it off.

As Fisher leaves, to take the train back to Uvalde via San Antonio, Thompson decides to join him.

Death waits behind a curtain. An autopsy will shatter the coroner's conclusions, and the presence of Winchester rifles will point directly to hidden assassins in the box seats.

Unanswered Questions

Did Ben Thompson and King Fisher meet in Austin by choice or by plan?

John King Fisher went to Austin on business (see time line). While in the capital, he met up with the notorious Ben Thompson. Some writers have made the accusation that the two met by plan. **Best Historical Guess**: The two met by pure chance and had a lot in common—including hard drinking. What started out as a lark, ended in tragedy.

Did King Fisher lure Ben Thompson into a trap?

Since Fisher and Joe Foster were close friends, some have speculated that Fisher may have lured Thompson to the Vaudeville to be murdered. But if true, why would Fisher be so close to Thompson when the shooting began? **Best Historical Guess**: Fisher mistakenly thought he could patch up differences between Foster and Thompson—and underestimated Thompson's ability to cause trouble. It cost him his life.

Was Ben Thompson assassinated?

The coroner's report stated that Thompson and Fisher were killed in a fight with Foster and Simms. But an autopsy of Thompson showed that the shooters were above and to the left of the victims—not right in front of them. **Best Historical Guess**: Two eyewitnesses to the fight, Alex T. Raymond and John R. Sublett, claimed Simms and Foster approached the sitting Thompson and Fisher. Thompson extended his hand, but Foster refused to shake it. Fisher spoke up and told Foster to shake hands with Thompson "like gentlemen." As Foster refused a second time, Simms and Coy quickly stepped aside. Reacting, Thompson and Fisher sprang from their seats as a fatal volley tore into them. Two of the fastest gunmen in the West never had a chance to pull their revolvers. Coy, with Thompson's pistol, and Simms, with his own, then fired additional shots into the dying men. Foster tried to draw his weapon and shot himself in the leg. The autopsy on Thompson's body confirmed that a volley of bullets struck him.

Historian Tom Bicknell believes, "once Thompson insisted on speaking to Foster, he sealed his doom." Bicknell also concludes, "Maybe if Ben hadn't pushed for a meeting with Foster, he may have gotten out of the Vaudeville alive. The shooters must have been ready to react to a given signal, and I believe this would have been when Simms and Coy moved quickly out of the way. Joe Foster was careful to be out of the line of fire. I doubt any argument had time to develop."

Quick on the Draw

"**Nitpickers and proponents of the "fast draw is a myth" crowd take note** [Fisher's] pistol was found belted around him, undischarged, and in his scabbard—a remarkable circumstance for one so quick in drawing and so self-possessed when in danger."

—The Daily News (Galveston), March 12, 1884

Aftermath: Odds & Ends

News of the shooting spread fast, reported Galveston's *The Daily News*. "Before the theatre was fairly cleared of its occupants, 1,500 people clamored at the closed doors of the building for admittance." The next day, the *San Antonio Express* reported that 3,000 more gathered that morning "to get a sight at the bodies."

⸺☆⸺

The physician attending to Joe Foster felt it was impossible to save his leg, so the leg was amputated "a short distance above the knee." Eleven days after the fight, on March 22, a doctor probing Foster's wound hit an artery and Foster bled to death. Foster's body was buried behind Jack Harris' grave in the city cemetery.

⸺☆⸺

Ben Thompson's brother Billy, who had been in San Antonio the night of the shooting, claimed the body to take home to Austin, Texas, via train. An autopsy performed in Austin stated that Thompson had been shot by eight bullets, five of them to the head. But the shocker was that some of the bullets removed from the body were Winchester rifle caliber. By the angle of trajectory, these bullets apparently had come from above and to the left, from the box seat area to the left of the dress circle (see diagram, p. 99). The evidence also suggested that the two victims were shot multiple times in the face after they were already down and helpless.

⸺☆⸺

King Fisher's body was shipped home to Uvalde, Texas, and buried. No autopsy was performed.

⸺☆⸺

Recommended: *Legendary Watering Holes: The Saloons that Made Texas Famous* edited by Richard Selcer, published by Texas A&M University Press; Look for Tom Bicknell's forthcoming book: *An Echo of Gunfire: The Forgotten Lives of Ben and Billy Thompson.*

FORT WORTH FIREFIGHT

LUKE SHORT vs LONG-HAIRED JIM COURTRIGHT

A COP WITH A CROOKED STREAK GETS NAILED

In the 1870s, Courtright wore his hair shoulder length and carried a brace of pistols in a red sash, a la Hickok.

FEBRUARY 8, 1887

Long-Haired Jim Courtright strides into the White Elephant Saloon in Fort Worth, Texas, and has words with co-owner Jake Johnson. Luke Short, the other owner, is called down from the game rooms and brought into the discussion.

The three men leave the saloon and walk down the sidewalk, stopping outside the Ella Blackwell shooting gallery. Courtright, owner of the T.I.C. Detective Agency, demands money for protection. Short demurs, claiming, with some authority, that he can protect himself without outside muscle.

Short has been standing with his thumbs in the armholes of his vest. When he drops his hands, an alarmed, Courtright says, "You needn't be getting out your gun."

Short replies, "I haven't got any gun here, Jim," raising up his vest to illustrate.

Courtright pulls out his own pistol but fails to pull the trigger (it is later learned that a cylinder jammed). Short fires his now-drawn gun and a bullet strikes Courtright; he then pumps four more bullets in Courtright as he falls.

This is the version of events as told by Johnson. If other issues were raised during the discussion, they died with Courtright.

Jim Courtright

Luke Short (above) is the undisputed top dog of high-stakes gambling in Fort Worth. The dapper gambler and gunman has ponied up and drawn inside straights in some of the West's most famous watering holes, including those found in Dodge City, Kansas, and Tombstone, Arizona. Now in partnership with Jake Johnson of the White Elephant Saloon, Short appeals to a genteel crowd of civic leaders and high rollers who frequent the game rooms upstairs to rub shoulders and match wits (and bets) with celebrity gamblers.

Long-Haired Courtright's Checkered Career

Controversial to say the least, James Timothy Isaiah Courtright was born in Iowa in 1848 and became a military scout, mining guard, ranch foreman and lawman. It was in this latter capacity, as city marshal of Fort Worth (1876-79), that he gained his most favorable reviews (he was the first city marshal to serve more than one term). In those days, he wore his hair shoulder length as was the style among scouts on the frontier. When his term as marshal expired,

he gravitated to Silver City, New Mexico, where he worked as a guard for the American Mining Company. After being implicated in several deaths, he fled back to Texas (he was later exonerated). Back in Fort Worth, Courtright opened the T.I.C. (for his initials) Detective Agency and, according to statements by Short and Johnson, was attempting to extort protection money when he was killed.

Daniel, 610 HOUSTON ST., FT. WORTH, TEXAS.

Aftermath: Odds & Ends

Luke Short was given a preliminary hearing and released on a $2,000 bond, but he never faced trial.

— ☆ —

Long-Haired Jim Courtright was given a big, fancy funeral. After he died, his children moved to California.

— ☆ —

In December 1890, Luke Short went to downtown Fort Worth to vent his indignation over what he considered a crooked gambling operation run by Charlie Wright. Short pulled out his pistol and demanded the dealers and gamblers "skin out." As Short turned over tables and broke up the hardware, Wright shot him with a shotgun from behind. Short, struck in his left leg and with part of his left thumb torn off, wheeled and snapped off a shot at the retreating Wright, fracturing his assailant's wrist.

— ☆ —

Shortly after the Wright affair, Short developed dropsy and died from the effects of the disease at a health spa in Geuda Springs, Kansas, on September 8, 1893.

— ☆ —

Recommended: *Jim Courtright of Fort Worth: His Life and Legend* by Robert K. DeArment, published by Fort Worth Christian University Press; and *Luke Short: A Biography* by his great-nephew Wayne Short, published by Devil's Thumb Press.

Luke Short (center) shot gambler Charley Storms in much the same fashion as he shot Long-Haired Jim Courtright. After an altercation at the Oriental Saloon in Tombstone in 1881, Storms attempted to accost Short outside. Short pulled iron and shot Storms in the heart point-blank, then shot him multiple times as he fell.

PIKE PEAKED!

KID CURRY VS PIKE LANDUSKY

TOWN'S NAMESAKE LAID LOW AS THE WILDEST OF THE WILD BUNCH TAKES OFF

Celebrating the holidays in Jacob "Jew Jake" Harris' saloon in newly named Landusky, Montana, the town's namesake, Powell "Pike" Landusky, is holding forth with his neighbors and friends at around 10:30 in the morning.

Melting snow has clogged the stove pipe in the store/saloon, and a young kid has been brought in to clean it out. Jew Jake hobbles around behind the bar on his one leg (the other was lost during a gunfight in Great Falls). He sets a bottle and glass on the bar in front of Landusky, who gets ready to take his first drink of the day.

Stepping in out of the cold, cowboys Lonie (pronounced LOne-E) Logan and Jim Thornhill, his neighboring rancher and partner, pass through the saloon into the clothing store. Their mission is to neutralize a gunman named Charles Hogan (a lunger). Thornhill orders 25 cents worth of apples as he and Lonie take up positions to handle Hogan when the fireworks start.

A few moments later, as planned, Harvey Logan, a.k.a. Kid Curry, comes in the front door. Kid Curry's younger brother John stays outside and guards the front door with a Winchester. Kid Curry advances straight toward Landusky and aggressively slaps him on the shoulder, knocking the bottle out of his hand. When Landusky turns, Kid Curry punches the noted brawler in the face with all his might.

When the two clinch, both Lonie and Thornhill step forward, yelling out, "Fair fight!" Landusky's friends, including Hogan, are intimidated and hold back from joining in.

As the men punch each other and scuffle, Kid Curry's pistol falls out of his coat pocket onto the floor. Thornhill fetches the Colt .45 by the barrel so no one can accuse him of assault. (Landusky's friends later allege Thornhill waved it at bystanders, warning, "The first man that makes a move will be killed.")

Landusky is a grizzled, experienced brawler. He gets the advantage on Kid Curry, landing on top of the smaller man while trying to gouge out his eyes. Kid Curry manages to get on top, pummeling the much bigger man until Landusky cries out "Enough!"

A mining friend of Landusky, Thomas Carter, asks Lonie to intercede, saying that Landusky has clearly had enough. Lonie allegedly replies, "He has not got enough for what he has done to us."

Thornhill finally convinces Kid Curry to let go of Landusky. The combatants stagger to their feet, and Landusky reaches in his coat and pulls out a semi-automatic pistol (an 1893 Borchardt). As he does, he calls Kid Curry a coward for attacking him without cause. (Landusky doesn't fire his pistol; one account claims he does, but either the gun misfired or he failed to chamber a round.)

Thornhill pitches the .45 to Kid Curry, who fires a shot in Landusky's gut. Curry fires three times in all, with two slugs hitting Landusky and one going awry. Landusky falls to the floor and dies in about five minutes.

Brother John rounds up the cowboys' wagon, and the four make their escape.

Harvey Logan, alias "Kid Curry," stands on the right in the famous Fort Worth Five photograph. Also shown is Butch Cassidy (seated, right) and the Sundance Kid (seated, left).

– ALL IMAGES TRUE WEST ARCHIVES –

Jim Thornhill (right of stove) throws a pistol to Kid Curry who shoots three times, striking Landusky twice. Everyone else heads for the back door. Notice the kid on the floor who was cleaning out the stove. (Inset) An 1893 semi-automatic 7.65x12mm Borchardt pistol.

Jew Jake's saloon explodes with violence as bystanders head for the back door.

Eyewitness Accounts

In the subsequent trial, eyewitnesses testified to the events leading up to Landusky's death. Here are a few of their statements:

The fight between Landusky and Harvey begins:

"When the fight started both Lonie Curry and Thornhill said to me: 'Hogan this is no fight of yours. This is a fight between them two' and I said 'all right.' There had been no guns drawn. Harvey Curry's gun fell out on the floor and Thornhill picked it up and held it in his hand and said 'no one shall interfere.'" —Thomas Smith Carter

Landusky appears to be defeated:

"Landusky offered no resistance except to try to keep Curry off with his hands. Landusky said take him off I have enough. Curry continued pounding him with his fist. Then he let Landusky up, did not hear anyone say let him up. Either Lonie Curry or Thornhill said the first man that makes a move I will kill him. After Landusky got up he reached to his right hand overcoat pocket and pulled something out but could not see what it was." [Note: Both combatants pulled out pistols from beneath their clothing, not from their gun belts.] —William McKenzie

Landusky calls Harvey a coward:

"Landusky gets up from the floor and says 'Kid you had no business to do this with me. Kid you are a coward.' At the same time he pulled a gun and Harvey Curry pulled his gun from his hip jacket. They both pointed their guns at each other. I heard a report of gun but don't know from what source, but Landusky threw down his hand and said, 'Oh, God,' I start to go out of the house and when I got to the door the second shot was fired. Landusky peeled sideways and fell on the floor. After I was outside there was one more shot fired making three.... Then Harvey Curry came out of the back door ... I heard Thornhill tell Curry to shoot."
—Edward Skilton

Harvey Logan (seen here with his soiled dove girlfriend, Annie Rogers) was by all accounts a good cowboy, but he was an avid reader of dime novels and was dead set on being a bad man. He more than succeeded.

> "Kid you had no business to do this with me. Kid you are a coward."
>
> —*Pike Landusky*

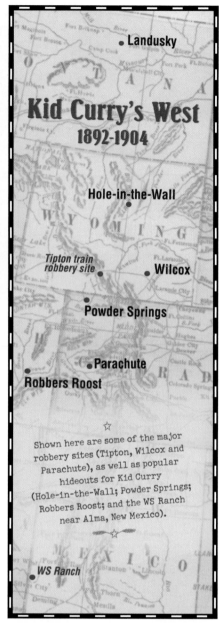

Kid Curry's West
1892-1904

Shown here are some of the major robbery sites (Tipton, Wilcox and Parachute), as well as popular hideouts for Kid Curry (Hole-in-the-Wall; Powder Springs; Robbers Roost; and the WS Ranch near Alma, New Mexico).

Christmas Day, 1894: Jew Jake (second from left) stands outside his saloon between big, bad Pike Landusky (third from left) and his stepdaughter Elfie (far left). The fourth person is believed to be Thomas Carter.

By all accounts, Pike Landusky liked to drink and mix it up in Jake's saloon.

On May 14, 1895, a jury found Lonie Logan not guilty in the death of Pike Landusky. More than two months later, a bench warrant was issued and served on Jim Thornhill. His case was dismissed without trial on December 2. Harvey "Kid Curry" Logan, having long fled the country, was never tried for Landusky's murder.

Harvey soon joined George "Flatnose" Currie's outlaw band, later merging with Butch Cassidy's so-called Wild Bunch. A string of rustling and train robberies followed. Harvey was finally captured in 1901, but he escaped jail in Knoxville, Tennessee. After another train robbery near Parachute, Colorado, on June 27 1904, lawmen surrounded the outlaw, and he killed himself rather than be recaptured.

Lonie apparently joined his brother at the Wild Bunch hangout, the Hole-in-the-Wall near the KC Ranch in Wyoming, and may have participated in the Wilcox, Wyoming, train robbery in 1899. In February 1900, Lonie returned to Dobson, Missouri, to visit an aunt who had raised him; a posse trapped and killed him there.

Jim Thornhill eventually sold his property in Landusky, Montana, and moved to Globe, Arizona, in 1916. He died there in the late 1920s.

Recommended: *Tiger of the Wild Bunch: The Life of Harvey "Kid Curry" Logan* by Gary A Wilson, published by Globe Pequot Press.

Probable Cause

When the time came for settlers to vote on a name for the fledgling community, the cowboys wanted Rock Creek and the miners wanted Landusky. The miners won.

The Logan brothers weren't big fans of Pike Landusky, who had borrowed a plow from them and allegedly returned it broken. Irritated, Harvey and Lonie delivered it back, tossing the worthless plow in Landusky's front yard.

Two months before the fight, Landusky stirred the pot. In October 1894, Harvey, his brother John and their brother-in-law Lee Self were arrested and charged with assault with a deadly weapon "without any considerable provocation." Although James Ross filed the claim, Harvey believed that the charges had been trumped up by his neighbor, Landusky. While Harvey was held on the assault charge, a deputized Landusky allegedly "beat Harvey unmercifully" and urinated on him.

To make matters more complicated, Lonie, a known ladies man, was sparking Landusky's stepdaughter Elfie.

The night before the fight, at a Christmas dance in John Logan's livery barn, Harvey and Landusky had words and they both agreed the next time they met, one of them would die.

ONE MAN WITH COURAGE MAKES A MAJORITY

JEFF MILTON
VS
THE BURT ALVORD GANG

"LOOK OUT FOR THE SON OF A BITCH, HE'S SHOOTING TO KILL."

Three-Fingered Jack gets three fingers full of buckshot in the gut from Jeff Milton's shotgun.

FEBRUARY 15, 1900

Today is supposed to be Wells Fargo Express Agent Jeff Milton's day off. But someone telegraphed in sick, so he is working the run from Nogales, Arizona, to Benson (see map, opposite page).

At dusk, when the train glides into the small station in Fairbank along the San Pedro River Valley, Jeff opens the express door to unload the packages bound for Tombstone and the surrounding area. As Jeff hands down the designated goods to the station agent, a cowboy on the platform yells out for Jeff to put up his hands.

"What's going on here?" Jeff asks an agent.

"Just a bunch of drunk cowboys having a joke, I guess," the agent replies.

"That kind of joke is liable to get somebody killed," says Jeff, as he continues unloading packages.

Five cowboys, who are using passengers on the platform as shields, show their weapons. One of them yells, "Throw up your hands and come out o' there!" With the command comes a rifle shot; the slug takes off Milton's hat.

Reaching behind the door of the express car, Milton appears with a sawed-off shotgun and barks back, "If there's anything here you want, come and get it." He quickly sizes up the situation though, realizing he can't return fire with the shotgun without hitting innocent people. Unfortunately, his pistol is on his desk, inside the car.

The five cowboys, still hiding behind passengers, open fire with high-powered rifles. The volley of shots from the outlaws shreds Milton's shirt as several shots strike his left arm between the elbow and shoulder, spinning him around and knocking him flat.

Thinking they have killed Milton, or at least knocked him out of the

The outlaws had good reason to fear Jeff Milton's resolve.

fight, the outlaws jump up into the doorway of the railroad car. Milton raises the shotgun with one hand and lets loose, hitting Jack Dunlap with pellets while another ball zings past Dunlap and hits Bravo Juan Yoas in the seat of his pants.

"Look out for the son of a bitch, he's shooting to kill," yells Dunlap, as he falls.

Milton's wound is serious (a slug has cut an artery). Faint from the loss of blood, Milton still has the presence of mind to kick the door shut and, at the same time, remove the keys to the safe from his pocket, flinging them into a pile of packages at the opposite end of the car. Cramming his wounded arm into the handle of a trunk, he rips the sleeve of his shirt at the cuff, tearing it to the shoulder, then twists his homemade tourniquet around his arm to stop the flow of blood spurting in his face. Before finishing, he passes out, landing in between the two trunks.

Outside, the outlaws circle the car and shoot round after round into it to ensure the death of Milton. After threatening the life of the engineer and using his body as a shield, the robbers climb into the car. One outlaw is about to shoot Milton, but the engineer stops him by pleading, "The man's dead now." The men search frantically for the keys but can't find them. In desperation, they round up their pard Dunlap and gallop off into the night with $40 in change.

The fight is over, but the race to save Milton's life has just begun.

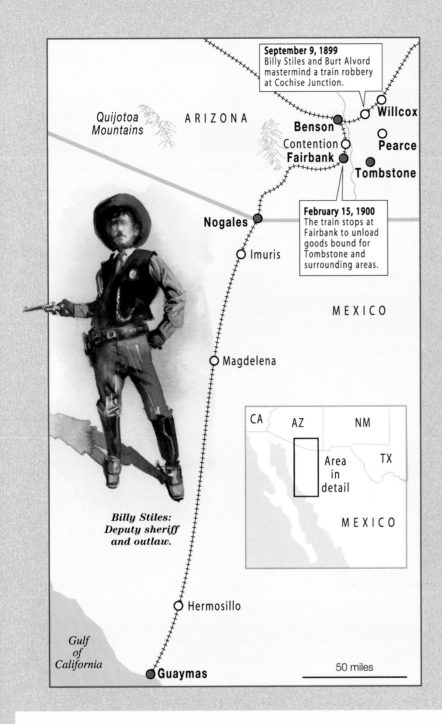

September 9, 1899
Billy Stiles and Burt Alvord mastermind a train robbery at Cochise Junction.

Quijotoa Mountains

ARIZONA

Willcox

Benson

Contention

Pearce

Fairbank

Tombstone

February 15, 1900
The train stops at Fairbank to unload goods bound for Tombstone and surrounding areas.

Nogales

Imuris

MEXICO

Magdelena

CA   AZ   NM

TX

Area
in
detail

MEXICO

**Billy Stiles:
Deputy sheriff
and outlaw.**

Hermosillo

*Gulf
of
California*

50 miles

Guaymas

The Race to Save Jeff Milton

After standing off five armed outlaws all by his lonesome, Jeff Milton is rushed to Benson where a special train arrives to transport him to the hospital in Tucson. An improvised tourniquet goes a long way in helping save Milton's life. At Saint Mary's hospital in the Old Pueblo, Dr. H.W. Fenner operates on Milton's shot-up arm, tying the bone with piano wire.

After nearly three hours under chloroform, Milton awakes in the night, thirsty for water. A young Mexican boy, assigned to watch over Milton, tells the lawman he is on strict orders not to give Milton any water.

"Listen here," the grizzled lawman hisses at the boy. "If you don't bring me some water, when I get up from here, I'm going to kill you."

The boy quickly brings a pitcher of water. Jeff drinks it all, calls for more and finishes three pitchers before his thirst is satiated. Then he sleeps eight hours.

A nurse arrives the next morning and notices Milton's gun under his pillow. The nurse reprimands him, "You can't keep that thing there." He replies, "Well, if I can't, I'll go to another hospital."

With the wound not healing properly, Dr. Fenner sends the lawman to San Francisco for treatment. By this time, Milton's arm is stinking and his left leg is swelled up to the size of his body. When the doctors at the Southern Pacific Hospital tell Milton to prepare his will because they are amputating his arm at the elbow, Milton tells them they aren't taking off his arm. He asks for the bill and pays it.

Someone chauffeurs him to Lane Hospital in San Francisco so he can be seen by Dr. Goodfellow, an old friend of his from Tombstone. Ordering Milton a whiskey, the doctor probes and cleans out the wound, fitting his patient with a brace to support his arm. Goodfellow predicts Milton will never use the arm again.

Milton throws the brace out the train window on his way back to Arizona. He fashions a buckskin bag with birdshot, which he ties to his wrist so he can constantly attempt to grab it with his bad hand. Over time, he is able to flex his hand, but he never does recover the free use of his arm.

A Clever Ruse Fails

The train robbers go out of their way to make sure Milton is far away from the action on the day of the robbery. The gang sends Billy Stiles to Nogales to tempt Milton with a story that a mining man wants to look at Jeff's claims out at the Quijotoa Mountains west of Nogales. They plan it for Milton's day off. To make doubly sure, Stiles asks Jeff to wire him from Nogales in case of any change in plans.

Milton does not get his day off though. He receives a telegram in Imuris, Sonora, from W.F. Overton of the express company, informing him that the messenger on duty is sick. Jeff forgets about his meeting with the mining speculator and mans his post through Nogales. The outlaws no doubt do a double-take when they see Milton—the very man they did not want to go up against—standing in the doorway of the express car in Fairbank.

New Breed of Lawless Lawmen

Nearly two decades after the Earps fled Arizona as fugitives, Tombstone had faded as a mining mecca. Speculators all moved up the road to Pearce, taking some buildings from Tombstone with them.

A new breed of lawmen worked both sides of the fence during that time in Cochise County. Burt Alvord, who grew up in Tombstone, was a well-known badman, which was why the town of Willcox hired him as a constable to police the boisterous cowboys in the area.

Alvord then hired Billy Stiles and Bill Downing as his deputies. Conspiring to leverage their newfound legality, Alvord gathered in local cowboys—including Matt Burts, the Owen brothers and Jack Dunlap— to rob some trains.

The gang's first robbery took place at Cochise Junction on September 9, 1899, when two men held up the train and got away with an untold amount of booty. Alvord and his men led the posses organized to chase those robbers and, of course, they found nothing. The second major robbery attempt occurred in Fairbank, but their well-laid plans to waylay Milton backfired. Then the posse out of Tombstone found Jack Dunlap where his partners had left him. He lived several days and "spilled the beans," implicating Matt Burts and confirming the suspicion that Burt Alvord, Billy Stiles and Bill Downing had backed the robbery.

Armed with Dunlap's confession, lawmen arrested the Owen brothers, Bob Brown, Downing, Stiles, Burts and Alvord. Stiles turned state's evidence, confessing he and Burts had committed the Cochise robbery and that Alvord and Downing had helped plan it. Released, Stiles went to Tombstone and busted Alvord out of jail.

At the request of Burt Mossman, the captain of the newly-formed Arizona Rangers, Alvord and Stiles helped capture Mexican bandit Augustin Chacon. Yet the duo ended up in the Tombstone jail once more. They escaped their cell on December 15, 1903, fleeing to Mexico, but Alvord would soon find himself back in jail. Lawmen caught him while he was riding with Stiles through the Nigger Head Gap on February 17, 1904.

Alvord finally served time in the pen (see mugshot), but it would not be the last time he saw the inside of a jail cell. He continued to ride a slippery journey through the gray area of the law.

A mugshot taken of Burt Alvord during one of his stints in prison.

A Confidential Report from the Arizona Rangers

Stiles and Alvord were still at it in 1906, according to a letter by Arizona Ranger H.H. McPhaul dated July 2 of that year. He warned authorities that the duo, lurking "near the Mexican line south of Yuma," intended to rob a train "on the [Southern Pacific] system."

The tip-off? The men were planning on placing water kegs along their escape route, intending to hold up "a train during the hot weather and with the aid of the water kegs outride and avoid any party sent after them," informants told McPhaul.

This never-before-published photo is labeled on the back, "Billy Stiles of Arizona," and was attached to the above-referenced Arizona Ranger report.

Jefff Milton, during his Texas Ranger days in the 1870s (left) and with his younger wife, Mildred Taitt Milton, outside their home in Tombstone (below). The background shows the Dragoon Mountains where the outlaws camped on the night before their robbery attempt in Fairbank.

A Good Man with a Gun

"Milton's Nerve" screamed the headline of an article about the express messenger's "brave stand" against overwhelming odds, published in the *Arizona Citizen* on February 16, 1900.

"He was extremely restless, but never nervous in danger" is how Milton's biographer, J. Evetts Haley, described him. "He was the agent of a proud and mighty land; he was always armed with the escutcheon of high honor. Not a pang of conscience ever plagued him. With a clean code, a sense of justice tempered with

fairness, and a mind quick in appraisal, he positively knew that right had always ridden close at his side."

During Milton's long career, he had gone up against scores of badmen including John Selman, John Wesley Hardin and Black Jack Ketchum.

When his wife Mildred noticed a bullet scar beneath his jaw, she inquired, "Jeff, who shot you there?" He replied, "A man who is not alive."

Aftermath: Odds & Ends

Bravo Juan Yoas fled to Mexico. After stopping in Cananea to have his wound dressed, Mexican officers spotted him and arrested him. They handed him over to the sheriff in Tombstone.

⸺ ☆ ⸺

Billy Stiles freely roamed around the West and was finally killed in Nevada in January 1908, while working as a deputy sheriff under the name William Larkin. Matt Burts was killed during a gunfight in Government Holes, California, in 1925. Bill Downing was killed in Willcox in 1908. Yoas supposedly died on the Amazon in 1910. Burt Alvord rambled around South America, and after a time in Brazil, he died of fever in the Barbados in 1910. When the Owen brothers died is unknown.

⸺ ☆ ⸺

Jeff Milton went from chasing outlaws on horseback as a Texas Ranger to jumping in a Model T Ford in 1917 at Tombstone, running down a bank robber and capturing him. He retired in 1930, due the rest after having served as a Ranger, range detective, mounted inspector along the Mexican border, rancher, prospector and oilman. After several years in Tombstone, he and his wife moved to Tucson, where he died at age 85 in May 1947.

⸺ ☆ ⸺

Recommended: *Jeff Milton: A Good Man with a Gun* by J. Evetts Haley, published by University of Oklahoma Press; and *Spawn Gone Wrong—The Odyssey of Burt Alvord: Lawman, Train Robber, Fugitive* by Don Chaput, published by Westernlore Press.

El tiene mas vidas
de un gato
(He has more lives
than a cat).

—Francisco Bedoya, about his old friend, Jeff Milton

SALT SIEGE SHOOT-OUT

☆

TEXAS RANGERS VS INSURRECTOS PASENOS

☆

"THEY KNEW NO LAW EXCEPTING THEIR GUNS."

☆

Insurgent snipers man the rooftops to rain fire down on the Texas Rangers' compound.

DECEMBER 13, 1877

At the Texas Ranger compound in San Elizario, Texas, Ranger Sgt. C.E. Mortimer walks down to El Molino (The Mill, see overview, p. 114) to check in on the Rangers stationed there.

On his way back to the barracks, a shot rings out from the roof of Nicholas Kohlaus' store and hits Mortimer in the back. The Ranger runs a few steps but falls. Firing breaks out on both sides as Lt. John B. Tays runs out from the barracks and pulls Mortimer to safety. (Mortimer dies three hours later.)

Charles Howard is the target of the shooters. He killed a popular local politician, Louis Cardis, who opposed Howard on ownership of the salt lakes. After agreeing to leave town, never to return, Howard did anyway—and is now under the protection of the Rangers.

Tays deploys men on the roof of the barracks, yet they are at a disadvantage as snipers on the roof of Mauro Lujan's house, 150 yards away, are slightly higher. One shot cuts the rim of merchant John Atkinson's hat as he hugs the roof and also gives Rocky Mathews a haircut. As the men attempt to cut a hole in the roof, Ranger John Eldridge chops off two of his fingers getting it done.

Several charges are beaten back, although Mathews later testifies, "[I] never saw a man after the first half hour's firing."

Two Rangers on the roof of El Molino pick off an insurgent as he raises his sombrero-clad head a little too high.

Around 4 p.m., the insurgents request a truce. Yet when Rangers attempt to retrieve blankets from the roof, insurgents fire at them. Firing continues sporadically throughout the night.

The next morning, insurgents charge the Rangers' corral but are once again beaten back by bullets. They make eight attempts to broach the Ranger defenses, but the able fighters inside hold them off. Attacks continue into the night, some say three. Insurgents even throw "rockets" into the hay of the Rangers' corral to start a fire (unsuccessfully).

The following day, December 15, insurgents try to flood the Ranger position but fail. So they begin tunneling under the headquarters to place explosives.

Mrs. Frank Campbell and her two children cross from the Ellis store (inside El Molino) to the Ranger barracks. Insurgents fire at them, but the three safely cross. She tells Tays the insurgents are breaking through a wall in Atkinson's store to get to Ranger Capt. Gregorio Garcia's men.

She asks Tays to leave the door open and have his men cover her husband and fellow ranger Frank Kent, so they can make a break for the barracks. The men safely cross and report that Capt. Garcia is wounded in the head and leg, and Miguel Garcia is also wounded.

Meanwhile, insurgents have discovered store owner Charles Ellis in a wine cellar. They jerk him out into the street and lasso him to a horse. They then drag him out of town where they slit his throat and leave him to bleed to death.

By Sunday, December 16, El Molino has fallen and the Rangers have lost the field of fire. Insurgents now brazenly run right up to the barracks and fire into the Rangers' own portholes. The Rangers abandon the front rooms and retreat to the rear of the building. As they do, their adversaries spring the "mine" they had dug, but the explosion does only minor damage to the structure.

Around 11 a.m., Tays raises a white flag. Pecos County Deputy Sheriff Andrew Loomis wants to leave. Tays steps outside to parlay with an emissary, who offers a ceasefire until morning, with negotiations to follow. Tays agrees. As the Rangers bed down, they can hear digging.

The next morning, faced with rifle pits built much closer to the barracks, the Rangers are ready to negotiate. Insurgent leader Francisco "Chico" Barela's offer: If Howard relinquishes his rights to the salt lakes, they will not hurt him.

Tays presents the terms to Howard, who wearily hangs his head, saying, "I will go, as it is the only chance to save your lives, but they will kill me."

He is right on both accounts.

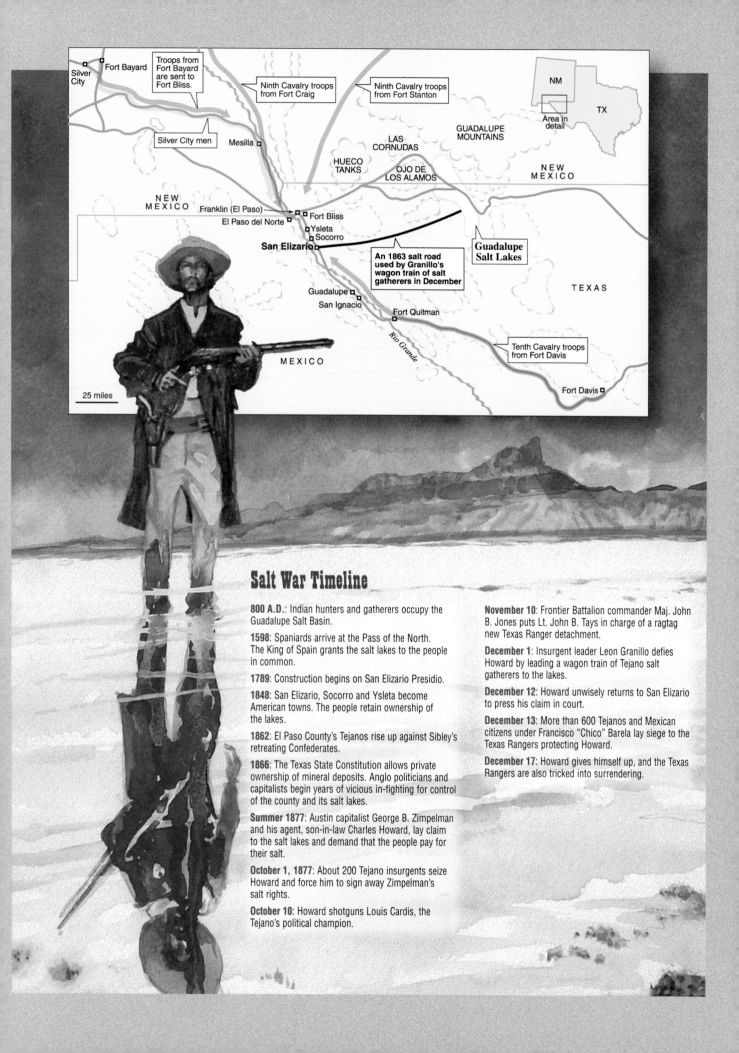

Silver City · Fort Bayard

Troops from Fort Bayard are sent to Fort Bliss.

Ninth Cavalry troops from Fort Craig

Ninth Cavalry troops from Fort Stanton

NM · TX · Area in detail

Silver City men · Mesilla

GUADALUPE MOUNTAINS

LAS CORNUDAS

HUECO TANKS

OJO DE LOS ALAMOS

NEW MEXICO

NEW MEXICO

Franklin (El Paso) · Fort Bliss

El Paso del Norte · Ysleta · Socorro

San Elizario

An 1863 salt road used by Granillo's wagon train of salt gatherers in December

Guadalupe Salt Lakes

TEXAS

Guadalupe · San Ignacio

Fort Quitman

Rio Grande

Tenth Cavalry troops from Fort Davis

MEXICO

Fort Davis

25 miles

Salt War Timeline

800 A.D.: Indian hunters and gatherers occupy the Guadalupe Salt Basin.

1598: Spaniards arrive at the Pass of the North. The King of Spain grants the salt lakes to the people in common.

1789: Construction begins on San Elizario Presidio.

1848: San Elizario, Socorro and Ysleta become American towns. The people retain ownership of the lakes.

1862: El Paso County's Tejanos rise up against Sibley's retreating Confederates.

1866: The Texas State Constitution allows private ownership of mineral deposits. Anglo politicians and capitalists begin years of vicious in-fighting for control of the county and its salt lakes.

Summer 1877: Austin capitalist George B. Zimpelman and his agent, son-in-law Charles Howard, lay claim to the salt lakes and demand that the people pay for their salt.

October 1, 1877: About 200 Tejano insurgents seize Howard and force him to sign away Zimpelman's salt rights.

October 10: Howard shotguns Louis Cardis, the Tejano's political champion.

November 10: Frontier Battalion commander Maj. John B. Jones puts Lt. John B. Tays in charge of a ragtag new Texas Ranger detachment.

December 1: Insurgent leader Leon Granillo defies Howard by leading a wagon train of Tejano salt gatherers to the lakes.

December 12: Howard unwisely returns to San Elizario to press his claim in court.

December 13: More than 600 Tejanos and Mexican citizens under Francisco "Chico" Barela lay siege to the Texas Rangers protecting Howard.

December 17: Howard gives himself up, and the Texas Rangers are also tricked into surrendering.

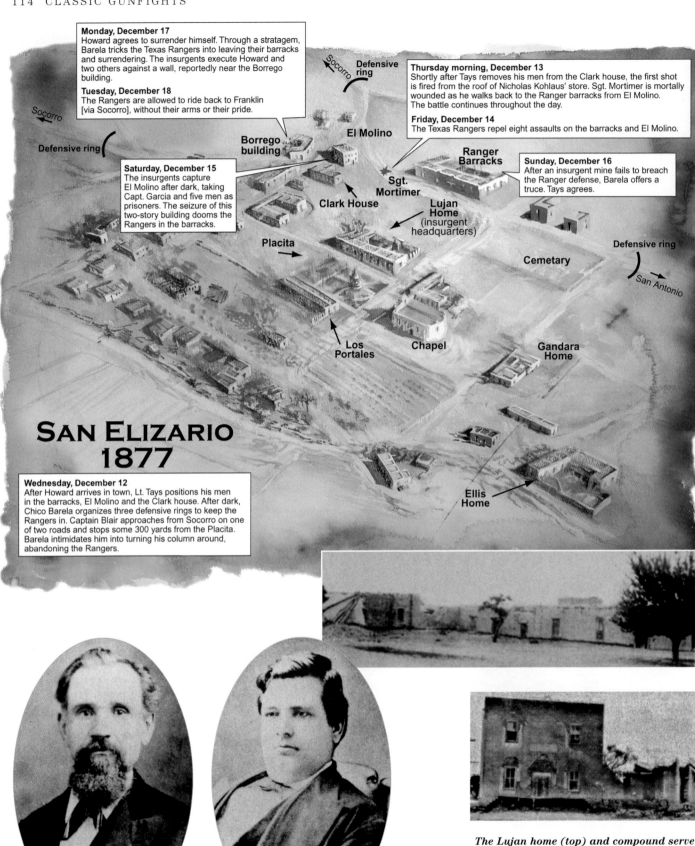

Monday, December 17
Howard agrees to surrender himself. Through a stratagem, Barela tricks the Texas Rangers into leaving their barracks and surrendering. The insurgents execute Howard and two others against a wall, reportedly near the Borrego building.

Tuesday, December 18
The Rangers are allowed to ride back to Franklin [via Socorro], without their arms or their pride.

Thursday morning, December 13
Shortly after Tays removes his men from the Clark house, the first shot is fired from the roof of Nicholas Kohlaus' store. Sgt. Mortimer is mortally wounded as he walks back to the Ranger barracks from El Molino. The battle continues throughout the day.

Friday, December 14
The Texas Rangers repel eight assaults on the barracks and El Molino.

Sunday, December 16
After an insurgent mine fails to breach the Ranger defense, Barela offers a truce. Tays agrees.

Saturday, December 15
The insurgents capture El Molino after dark, taking Capt. Garcia and five men as prisoners. The seizure of this two-story building dooms the Rangers in the barracks.

Socorro

Defensive ring

Socorro

Defensive ring

Borrego building

El Molino

Ranger Barracks

Sgt. Mortimer

Clark House

Lujan Home (insurgent headquarters)

Placita

Cemetary

Defensive ring

San Antonio

Los Portales

Chapel

Gandara Home

SAN ELIZARIO 1877

Wednesday, December 12
After Howard arrives in town, Lt. Tays positions his men in the barracks, El Molino and the Clark house. After dark, Chico Barela organizes three defensive rings to keep the Rangers in. Captain Blair approaches from Socorro on one of two roads and stops some 300 yards from the Placita. Barela intimidates him into turning his column around, abandoning the Rangers.

Ellis Home

The Lujan home (top) and compound serve as the insurgent headquarters for most of the fight. El Molino (above) houses two "American" stores: the Ellis Store and the Atkinson Store. Both owners lose their lives. Ironically, prior to the fight, John Atkinson sold his store and liquidated his assets, and was planning to leave town.

Louis Cardis (at left) and Charles Howard (at right) both die tragically.

– COURTESY UNIVERSITY OF TEXAS EL PASO –

Faces of the Insurgency

Acabenlos! (Finish them!)

The Tejanos (Texans of Mexican descent) who fight at San Elizario successfully overthrow the local government in El Paso County for 84 days and force the surrender of 20 Texas Rangers. As many as 650 men bore arms, 20 to 30 died and scores more were wounded.

Led by "Chico" Barela, the ragtag insurgency boasts Indian fighters and former Rangers, although most are farmers and vaqueros. They are brave and determined men, but from the Texas Rangers' point of view, the insurgents are one step above a mob.

Barela tells Lt. Tays that Howard is safe so long as he relinquishes all claims to the salt lakes. Having convinced Howard to surrender, Tays accompanies Howard and Atkinson (who joins them as a translator) to the Gandara home where Barela shrewdly separates the trio. Howard and Tays are held in one room, while Atkinson is isolated and persuaded to fork over the $11,000 of assets he is carrying. He agrees on the condition that he, Howard, McBride and all the Rangers will depart without molestation. Atkinson is also assigned the task of writing out an agreement for the Rangers' surrender (Tays is in another room and isn't privy to any of this).

Sent to the Ranger compound, Atkinson tells the Rangers that Lt. Tays has "ordered" them to go down "with [their] arms" as they are "wanted as witnesses, and that all [has] been peaceably settled."

Using Atkinson as a wedge, Barela has successfully convinced the Rangers at the compound to give up the fight.

Once the Rangers walk out and they are disarmed, the junta leaders decide to execute Howard, Atkinson and McBride. One at a time, the three are walked to a wall near the Borrego building and shot. Atkinson brings up Barela's promises, but the crowd shouts, "Acabenlos!" (Finish them!). The insurgents hack their bodies to pieces and throw them down an abandoned well.

The gathered crowd is not satisfied and begins demanding the lives of all anglos. To his credit, Barela convincingly threatens them with bodily harm, and they desist. But even Barela can't stop the subsequent looting, which spreads to even the stores of Tejanos who support the insurgency.

In the end, Chico Barela rises to leadership in a crisis, then fades into obscurity. Unlike the stereotypical portrait of the insurgent leader, he is described as, "a quiet man, fair for a Mexican, with brown hair and blue eyes."

Capt. Thomas Blair

**El Paso Sheriff
Charles Kerber**

Texas Ranger Lt. John B. Tays

A good example of the gear and dress of the Rangers at San Elizario is this circa 1878 photo of Texas Rangers Andy and Tom Zickefoose, with an unidentified man in the middle. This is the only known photo taken of Salt War Rangers.

— COURTESY LARRY WAYNE ZICKEFOOSE —

Motley Crew of Rangers

Texas Ranger Lt. John B. Tays (left) makes a serious tactical mistake when he leaves the Ranger compound with Howard to discuss terms of a settlement. He separates himself from his command and does not provide instructions for the Rangers left behind. Everything unravels when Barela shrewdly detains Lt. Tays in another room, then promises Atkinson freedom if he goes back to the compound and convinces the Rangers there that he has bought their freedom. Exhausted and unsure of what to do with Tays gone, they comply. Once outside, they are surrounded and disarmed. Thus, Company C becomes the only Texas Ranger outfit ever to surrender.

The unit was formed only months before, when authorities in Austin ordered Maj. John B. Jones of the Frontier Battalion of Texas Rangers to go to El Paso and form a unit of 20 men to deal with the growing crisis there. Although an excellent judge of men, Jones took whoever he could get. They were undoubtedly decent fighters, but their training was nil. Jones found these men through an ad he ran in the *Mesilla Valley Independent*, stating his intention of "recruiting a company to put down the El Paso County mob. Reliable men with horse and Winchester rifle will be paid $40 per month and board. Here is a chance to serve your county!"

Communication Breakdown

1. Pleas for help come from El Paso County to Gov. Richard Hubbard in Austin, Texas.
2. Hubbard contacts President Hayes in Washington, D.C.
3. Hayes contacts Secretary of War George W. McCrary, also in Washington.
4. McCrary contacts Gen. William T. Sherman, also in Washington.
5. Sherman contacts Gen. Philip Sheridan in Chicago.
6. Sheridan contacts Maj. Gen. John Pope at Fort Leavenworth, Kansas, and
7. Maj. Gen. O.O. Ord in San Antonio.
8. Pope sends orders to Col. Edward Hatch in Santa Fe, New Mexico.
9. Ord sends orders to Col. Andrews at Fort Davis.

Where Was the Cavalry?

Thanks to the modern marvel of electromagnetic communication (the telegraph), officials in Washington and elsewhere (see map, above) were in immediate communication about the situation at San Elizario. Even though the U.S. Army committed troops from every available post within a 200-mile radius, no one arrived in time to save the lives of Howard and the others.

The most damning aspect of the siege is that Capt. Blair was in the county with about 20 troops when the fighting started. He marched with his men to San Elizario on December 12, but he was intercepted by Chico Barela and a large group of insurgents just outside town (some reports say within 300 yards of the plaza). Barela intimidated him into retreating back to Franklin. Blair then wired his superiors a series of reports covering his tail (and lack of direct action), and remained there until after the executions.

Colonel Edward Hatch arrived in Franklin with another company or two (very small outfits). He had intended to wait until the other six or seven companies arrived, but he decided to move quickly down the valley. He made it all the way to San Elizario with 54 men, but most of the insurgents had already fled. Meanwhile, the Texas Rangers and Silver City rogue civilian outfit moved down the valley behind him and avenged the executions by killing civilians and several insurgents who had remained behind.

In Washington, Chicago and Fort Leavenworth, the frustrated generals couldn't figure out what the delay was in getting the army into action.

Spooked!
Chico Barela meets the Blair detachment and intimidates them into turning around and going back to Franklin. This is the deciding factor in the fates of the Rangers and Howard.

Aftermath: Odds & Ends

On December 18, the Texas Rangers were released, without their firearms. They vowed vengeance. Most of the insurgents flee to Mexico.

☆

Colonel Edward Hatch arrived on December 21 with lead elements of the Ninth Cavalry, as did 30 Silver City Volunteers led by John Kinney and Grant County Deputy Sheriff "Dangerous Dan" Tucker.

☆

El Paso Sheriff Charles Kerber led the Rangers and Silver City men on a killing spree in Ysleta and Socorro before Col. Hatch put a stop to the mayhem.

☆

Major hostilities ended by 1878, yet guerrilla activity and crime continued to plague El Paso County.

☆

In 1879, Benito Gonzales, the new sheriff, and George W. Baylor, El Paso's new Texas Ranger commander, tacitly decided not to pursue anyone further for Salt War crimes. Slowly, the Salt War faded into the past. The shame of the Texas Rangers' surrender is still felt to this day.

☆

Recommended: *Salt Warriors: Insurgency on the Rio Grande* by Paul Cool, forthcoming from Texas A&M University Press.

BEYOND CUSTER HILL

---   ☆   ---

CUSTER AND THE SEVENTH CAVALRY VS 2,000 INDIANS

---   ☆   ---

Custer: Everything that can go wrong, does.

JUNE 25, 1876

George Armstrong Custer's mind is racing with military strategies and tactics. As usual, he is reacting to a fluid battle situation (something at which he's a genius).

After ordering Maj. Marcus Reno to attack a large Indian village nestled in Montana's Little Bighorn Valley, Custer notices 50 "hostiles" on his right flank and gives chase. When they scatter, Custer keeps going, leading his command north. As he rides, he formulates a new battle plan without telling his other commanders (this is one of Custer's biggest faults as a leader).

Now he's looking for a river crossing as his battalion continues north at a gallop along the barren shoulders of the Little Bighorn River (see map, opposite page).

The regiment turns into a broad, fantail ravine and follows it down. As they traverse the gully, Custer's command starts taking fire from the rear. Wolf Tooth, a Cheyenne who had been scouting with 40 to 50 warriors, sees the soldiers heading for the village and opens fire.

With Indians behind him, Custer cannot commit his entire command, so he sends Algernon Smith and E Troop to test the crossing. Meanwhile, Custer and four companies hang back, riding the ridgeline above the river as a rear guard.

On Smith's return, Custer learns that the ford at Dry Creek (a.k.a. Muskrat Creek) is "too miry" and full of bogs. A small number of warriors (believed to be four) are defending this crossing from the village side, but more important, Smith notes that the Indians, mostly noncombatants, are fleeing to the west and northwest. This is Custer's worst fear: that the inhabitants of the camp will escape.

Now Custer is even more determined to find a crossing that will head off the fleeing Indians.

Wolf Tooth and his warriors continue harassing and sniping at the troops from long range, but Custer is not yet worried. He has been in hundreds of fights during his storied Civil War career and is considered by some to be the top Indian fighter in the U.S. Army.

> **[** This is Custer's worst fear: that the inhabitants of the camp will escape. **]**

Custer leaves three of his five companies—I, C and L—fighting Wolf Tooth's men (and to act as a connection when Capt. Frederick Benteen and the pack train come up). With Companies E and F, Custer rides northwest off the ridgeline and into a broad plain that empties toward the river. As Custer and his troops approach the river bank, they are fired on by a group of warriors who are guarding the women and children.

Members of F Company dismount and form a skirmish line. Instead of having his troopers each hold three horses (see 1876 cavalry tactics, p. 121), Custer orders more firepower on the ground and has them each hold eight horses (a bold but risky technique he used on the Yellowstone three years earlier). Indians waving blankets and shooting cause the soldiers' horses to stampede. Warriors quickly capture them. With most of F Troop on foot, Custer knows the entire operation and his command are in grave peril.

While Custer attempts this second crossing, word is sent to the warriors fighting Reno that soldiers are trying to capture the women and children. Virtually all the Indian combatants in the Reno sector disengage and race pell-mell toward the slopes above the north end of the village.

Meanwhile, F Company is retreating back toward the ridgeline, where the rest of the command has gathered, as Company E (which still has its horses) lays down covering fire. After a one-mile run, F Company finally gains the top of a ridge. E Company dismounts and fights in a skirmish line to cover its horseless comrades. A 20-minute gunfight ensues

Continued on p. 120

Superior firepower keeps the Indians at bay for the first hour of the fight. Wolf Tooth and his warriors stay way back in the tall grass, away from the long range of the soldier's Springfields. (The .45-70 caliber trapdoor carbines can accurately fire 300 yards beyond a Winchester.) As more and more warriors spill onto the battlefield from the Reno sector, however, the Custer skirmishers are overwhelmed as increasing numbers of Indians stalk them in the tall grass. The Indians have at least 200 repeating rifles (according to archaeologists).

How Big is the Indian Village?

Custer and his officers first get a good look at the Sioux and Cheyenne's encampment from a distant ridge (see 5 on map). The camp is big, but it is not as large as many reports will later indicate. Although Black Elk later testifies that it was the biggest Indian village he had ever seen, Benteen's estimate of 10,000 Indians in the camp is likely a gross exaggeration. Benteen has several motives for embellishing the truth: a huge enemy encampment helps cover his lack of action, and the inflated numbers may encourage Congress to stop military cuts.

One problem in estimating the village's size is that when the attack occurs, Indians begin fleeing with their tipis. After the battle, the warriors move their camp 1.5 miles north of the old village site. The troops who later investigate the battleground assume the village is three miles long when in reality, they are seeing two village locations.

Most historians today estimate the hostiles' strength at 2,000 warriors, which is almost a 10-to-one ratio against Custer's 210 soldiers.

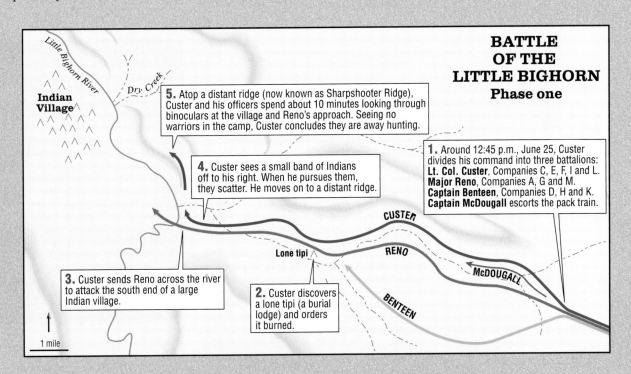

BATTLE OF THE LITTLE BIGHORN Phase one

Little Bighorn River

Dry Creek

Indian Village

5. Atop a distant ridge (now known as Sharpshooter Ridge), Custer and his officers spend about 10 minutes looking through binoculars at the village and Reno's approach. Seeing no warriors in the camp, Custer concludes they are away hunting.

1. Around 12:45 p.m., June 25, Custer divides his command into three battalions: **Lt. Col. Custer**, Companies C, E, F, I and L. **Major Reno**, Companies A, G and M. **Captain Benteen**, Companies D, H and K. **Captain McDougall** escorts the pack train.

4. Custer sees a small band of Indians off to his right. When he pursues them, they scatter. He moves on to a distant ridge.

CUSTER

RENO

McDOUGALL

Lone tipi

BENTEEN

3. Custer sends Reno across the river to attack the south end of a large Indian village.

2. Custer discovers a lone tipi (a burial lodge) and orders it burned.

1 mile

Why Does Custer Believe the Village is Empty of Warriors?

"Then Custer halted his command on the high ridge about 10 minutes, and officers looked at the village through glasses. Saw children and dogs playing among the tepees but no warriors or horses except few ponies grazing around. There was then a discussion among the officers as to where the warriors might be and someone suggested that they might be buffalo hunting, recalling that they had seen skinned buffalo along the trail on June 24. Custer now made a speech to his men saying, 'We will go down and make a crossing and capture [not kill] the village.' The whole command then pulled off their hats and cheered. And the consensus of opinion seemed to be among the officers that if this could be done the Indians would have to surrender when they would return, in order not to fire upon their women and children."

—John Martin, the last trooper to see Custer alive

Do Eager Beavers Doom Custer?

Mary Crawler, one of the Indian participants, says, "Custer's men got to the river above the beaver dam where the water is deep." She goes on to explain that the ford at Dry Creek was flooded out because of a beaver dam downstream, and that the Indians knew to cross below the dam.

Beaver lodge, on the Missouri by Karl Bodmer.

– COURTESY LIBRARY OF CONGRESS –

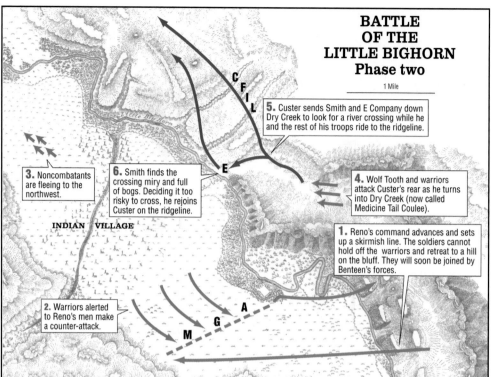

BATTLE OF THE LITTLE BIGHORN Phase two

1 Mile

5. Custer sends Smith and E Company down Dry Creek to look for a river crossing while he and the rest of his troops ride to the ridgeline.

3. Noncombatants are fleeing to the northwest.

6. Smith finds the crossing miry and full of bogs. Deciding it too risky to cross, he rejoins Custer on the ridgeline.

4. Wolf Tooth and warriors attack Custer's rear as he turns into Dry Creek (now called Medicine Tail Coulee).

1. Reno's command advances and sets up a skirmish line. The soldiers cannot hold off the warriors and retreat to a hill on the bluff. They will soon be joined by Benteen's forces.

INDIAN VILLAGE

2. Warriors alerted to Reno's men make a counter-attack.

Continued from p. 118

while Custer desperately tries to stall until the pack train and reinforcements arrive. (Custer's brother Boston has told him both are six miles away.)

> ### "Militarily, it finally makes sense to me."
>
> —*Col. Michael D. Mahler U.S. Army retired*

As the Indians become increasingly bolder, more and more cavalry horses are stampeded and captured. A charge by C Company to drive back some of the newly arriving Indians meets with disaster as the soldiers are cut off and surrounded. Half of Company C's soldiers die, and panic sets in all along the skirmish line as troopers bunch together and begin to run.

With over half of his command unhorsed, Custer realizes his only hope is for Capt. Benteen and Maj. Reno to save him.

Helplessly watching the collapse of his command, Custer and his headquarters staff kill horses to make breastworks on the highest point of

a hillock. Panicked soldiers begin running toward the hill as Indian suicide riders step up their bold attacks.

As if things could not get any worse for Custer, most of the warriors (an estimated 1,500) who were fighting Reno now come pouring onto the battlefield from the south, across the bluffs, through the water and up all the draws and coulees.

Company E holds a position west and below Custer's location to protect Custer's flank from warriors who are moving in from the northwest. In spite of this, suicide warriors successfully get past Company E and stampede all of the troopers' remaining horses.

A two-hour gun battle that started slowly now gains a frightening momentum as waves of warriors on horseback and on foot quickly overrun the few able soldiers on the hilltop with Custer and kill them all.

With some 190 dead and dying soldiers strewn for hundreds of yards, the warriors turn their attention to the 15-20 men from Company E, who are surrounded, on foot and out of ammunition. Gamely, these men make a run for it, many still carrying their empty weapons to use as clubs. They are all chased into a deep ravine and killed. The battle is over.

The controversy begins.

Custer, in 1873, wearing the exact outfit he is thought to have worn at the Little Bighorn battle (he took off the buckskin jacket just prior to the battle). He is also holding the same rifle he carried, a Remington Rolling Block.

1876 U.S. Cavalry Tactics & Strategies

In 1874, Emory Upton codified new cavalry tactics in a manual that incorporated a "set of fours" as the basic cavalry unit, or squad.

Unlike in movie portrayals, cavalrymen in the 1870s seldom fired from horseback. Instead, cavalry companies (38 to 44 men in Custer's case) dismounted and spread out in a skirmish line. One man from each squad gathered up the dismounted troopers' horses and held them in the rear. The dismounted skirmishers knelt for steadier aim.

In the case of the Little Bighorn battle, only one company at a time is deployed in a skirmish line, with the remainder held in reserve. For the first hour of fighting, this single dismounted company (L Company) effectively holds the Indians in check. It is only after the warriors from the Reno fight creep onto the Custer battlefield (the tall grass provided perfect cover) that the Indians are able to isolate the skirmishers and overwhelm them.

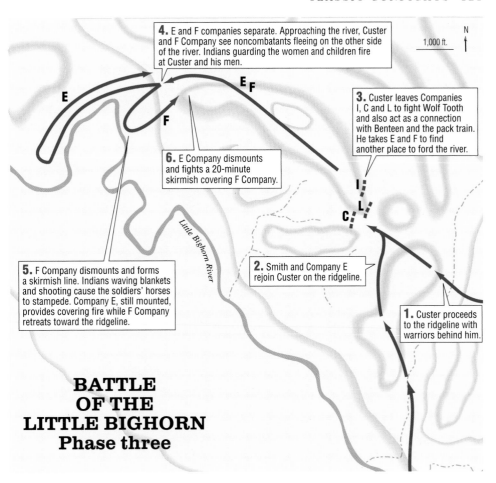

4. E and F companies separate. Approaching the river, Custer and F Company see noncombatants fleeing on the other side of the river. Indians guarding the women and children fire at Custer and his men.

3. Custer leaves Companies I, C and L to fight Wolf Tooth and also act as a connection with Benteen and the pack train. He takes E and F to find another place to ford the river.

6. E Company dismounts and fights a 20-minute skirmish covering F Company.

5. F Company dismounts and forms a skirmish line. Indians waving blankets and shooting cause the soldiers' horses to stampede. Company E, still mounted, provides covering fire while F Company retreats toward the ridgeline.

2. Smith and Company E rejoin Custer on the ridgeline.

1. Custer proceeds to the ridgeline with warriors behind him.

1,000 ft.

N

Little Bighorn River

BATTLE OF THE LITTLE BIGHORN
Phase three

Dismounted troopers establish a skirmish line as the "led horses" are taken over the hill for safekeeping. This backfires when Chief Gall and other warriors sneak up on them and stampede the horses.

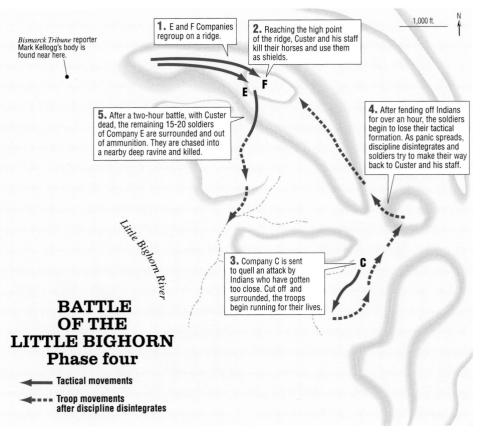

Bismarck Tribune reporter Mark Kellogg's body is found near here.

1. E and F Companies regroup on a ridge.

2. Reaching the high point of the ridge, Custer and his staff kill their horses and use them as shields.

5. After a two-hour battle, with Custer dead, the remaining 15-20 soldiers of Company E are surrounded and out of ammunition. They are chased into a nearby deep ravine and killed.

4. After fending off Indians for over an hour, the soldiers begin to lose their tactical formation. As panic spreads, discipline disintegrates and soldiers try to make their way back to Custer and his staff.

3. Company C is sent to quell an attack by Indians who have gotten too close. Cut off and surrounded, the troops begin running for their lives.

1,000 ft.

N

Little Bighorn River

BATTLE OF THE LITTLE BIGHORN
Phase four

◄——— **Tactical movements**

◄--- **Troop movements after discipline disintegrates**

A Trio of Warriors, Custer's Crow Scouts:

(From top) Mitch Bouyer the interpreter; Hairy Moccasin; and Goes Ahead.

White Man Runs Him (above) later turns on Curly and claims that Curly fled before the battle.

After the Battle of the Rosebud on June 17, Sitting Bull (right) performs the Sun Dance. Afterwards, he has visions of soldiers falling from the sky. Eight days later, Custer and his men are defeated at the Little Bighorn.

(Opposite) The Crow scout Curly, the most famous of all the scouts with Custer.

Seventh U.S. Cavalry Officers of the Black Hills Expedition, August 1874, the day before marching to Fort Abraham Lincoln. Killed in action at the Little Bighorn are, from left: (1) Capt. George W. Yates (2) First Lt. Donald McIntosh (3) First Lt. Tom Custer (4) Second Lt. Henry M. Harington (5) First Lt. James Calhoun (Custer's brother-in-law) (6) Lt. Col. George A. Custer (7) Crow Scout Bloody Knife (8) First Lt. Algernon E. Smith (9) Second Lt. Benjamin H. Hodgson. Later charged with supervising the transfer of Custer's remains from the battlefield to West Point, (10) Maj. Joseph G. Tilford is seated nearby.

– COURTESY OF ROBERT M. UTLEY –

Custer's Black Hills Expedition (below), which ultimately leads to the fight on the Little Bighorn. That's George, left of center in foreground, in light buckskins.

Custer's last photo, taken in April, two months before his death.

Did Custer Save the Last Bullet for Himself?

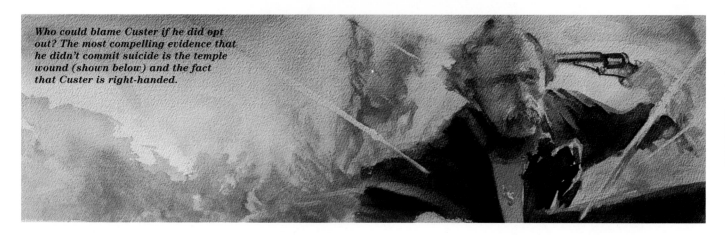

Who could blame Custer if he did opt out? The most compelling evidence that he didn't commit suicide is the temple wound (shown below) and the fact that Custer is right-handed.

Two days after the fight, on June 27, relief troops finally take a look at the Custer battlefield. Peering through binoculars from the Little Bighorn Valley floor, Lt. James Bradley thinks he sees skinned buffalo. Captain Thomas Weir later remarks, "My God, how white they look!" Of course, the white patches they all see glittering in the distance are the stripped and mutilated bodies of George Armstrong Custer and his entire command.

Custer's body is found amid a knot of slain men and horses just below the western summit of a small hill. Lieutenant Edward Godfrey and another soldier count 42 bodies strewn across the slope.

"We found no powder burns," Godfrey later reports about Custer's body, implying he didn't commit suicide. (When a gun is fired close to the body, it leaves powder burns.) Godfrey and others claim that besides two bullet wounds, Custer has "not been touched." This is a blatant lie, which Godfrey later admits in a letter to a friend. His motive for lying, he states, is to spare Custer's wife, Elizabeth, further grief.

In the letter, Godfrey confesses that Custer's left thigh was slashed to the bone (Indians believed that it would impede mounting a horse in the afterlife); a finger was severed; and an arrow shaft was shoved into Custer's penis.

So Did He or Didn't He?

If Godfrey was lying about the mutilation of Custer, should we trust his statement about the powder burns? Or was he trying to spare Elizabeth and the nation from the trauma of knowing Custer killed himself?

Custer had two bullet wounds, Godfrey

reported. He was struck with a bullet near his left temple and another in his ribs, near the heart. Tellingly, the rib wound and thigh slash were bloodless, while the temple wound was bloody. The wounds indicated that the head shot happened first because Custer's heart was still pumping blood. By the time someone shot him near the heart, he was already dead (so scratch all the paintings of Custer standing and holding his side).

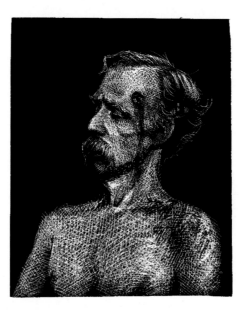

"The odds of being shot in the temple in a battle are astronomical. It has always seemed like a classic case of suicide to me," says John Wagner, a Vietnam veteran, retired police lieutenant and longtime Custer buff.

Most Custer historians are just as emphatic that it wouldn't have been in Custer's nature to commit suicide. "I do not

believe Custer committed suicide," Michael Donahue says. "He was a soldier who had many close calls and he would have felt it a cowardly act. He also was right-handed and the bullet entered his left temple. Godfrey looked for evidence of suicide and saw none. Custer's younger brother Boston and nephew Harry were his responsibility. I believe they fled after George's death. They were found 100 yards below Custer Hill dead and mutilated. Custer would never have allowed this if he had been alive and [he] could not have killed himself in front of them."

One item is not in dispute: on the frontier, virtually all soldiers—including Custer—had an agonizing dread of being captured alive by Indians.

Before his death, Custer wrote about Indian torture in his autobiography and repeated the oft-mentioned refrain that officers "asserted they would never be taken alive by Indians."

This pervasive belief, that the worst thing that could happen was to be captured alive by Indians, played into the collapse and rout of Custer's men.

Add to the command's tortured mindset the conditions on that hot June day, and it's not hard to imagine that when Custer's soldiers were overrun, they might have fallen victim to their own lurid indoctrination. And in that light, it is not hard to imagine that Custer either shot himself, or that his brother Tom, or someone else close to him, pulled the trigger.

The Killing Ground, Three Years Later

In 1879, Capt. George Sanderson and his 11th Infantry were sent out to the battlefield to clean it up. Photographer Stanley Morrow accompanied them, and he captured this grisly scene of bones and equipment, still strewn across the hills and gullies. In the foreground are a soldier's boot soles. The Indians had no use for the soles and would cut off the bottoms and keep the tops for pouches or other uses.

There is only one known earlier photo taken of Last Stand Hill in 1877 by Fouch. In this photo, the horses' skulls still have hair. The photo is in a private collection.

Custer's Horses

Custer had two horses with him on the campaign: Vic (Victory) and Dandy. In battle, he rode Vic (at right), who had a white blaze on his face and three white stockings. Historian Michael Donahue believes the Indians took Vic with them to Canada. In contrast, one field report stated that Vic was found dead, 100-150 feet from Custer, and another stated Vic was one of the dead horses making up the breastworks near where Custer died. Dandy (at left) was with the pack train and not only survived, but was also sent back to the Custer family.

Aftermath: Odds & Ends

The total annihilation of George Armstrong Custer's men did not end the fighting. The Sioux and Cheyenne warriors on Custer Hill immediately swarmed back to Maj. Marcus Reno's and Capt. Frederick Benteen's position, and attacked them with everything they had. "The bullets fell like a perfect shower of hail," Lt. Francis Gibson remembered. Benteen took control and rallied the men in their makeshift, horseshoe-shaped defensive line. In spite of Reno taking 73 more casualties (13 killed, 60 wounded), the surviving Seventh Cavalry soldiers held off the Indians for almost two days. Late on June 26, the Sioux and Cheyennes drifted away and an eerie silence overtook the Little Bighorn Valley.

* ☆ *

The Indians went their separate ways, with Sitting Bull and his band taking refuge in Canada. Crazy Horse and others headed toward the nearby Rosebud country and wherever else they could find buffalo.

* ☆ *

A shocked nation demanded answers and results. The U.S. Army under Gen. Philip Sheridan redoubled its efforts to find and capture the Indians, but for the most part, the soldiers were unsuccessful. General George Crook, however, did claim a victory over Chief American Horse and the Brule Sioux at the battle of Slim Buttes in September.

* ☆ *

Recommended: *Archaeology, History, and Custer's Last Battle* by Richard A. Fox, Jr., published by University of Oklahoma Press; *Custer in '76* edited by Kenneth Hammer, published by University of Oklahoma Press; *The Custer Myth* by Col. W.A. Graham, published by Stackpole Books; and *Indian Views of the Custer Fight* by Richard G. Hardorff, published by Arthur H. Clark Company.

Credit Where Credit is Due

*This book is dedicated to
my Grandmother,
Louise Robinson Guess Swafford.
She lit the fire and kept it stoked
with stories of our outlaw relatives.*

Design and Computer Graphics

Robert Ray, Dan Harshberger, Gus Walker and Abby Pearson

Cover Design

Dan Harshberger

Editing

Meghan Saar, who spends countless hours getting the words right.

Special Thanks to these Exemplary Researchers & Authors

Black Bart: Bill Secrest, Sr., George Hoeper; **Wham Robbery:** Larry Upton, Larry D. Ball; **The Talbot Gang and Caldwell:** Rod Cook, Robert K. DeArment; **The Alamo:** Paul Hutton, Dan Kilgore, Bill Groneman, Gary Zaboly, Richard G. Santos, Stephen L. Hardin, Alan C. Huffines; **Billy the Kid:** Frederick Nolan; **Butch & Sundance:** Dan Buck, Anne Meadows, Donna Ernst; **Tiburcio Vasquez:** Bill Secrest, Sr., John Boessenecker, who also provided expertise on Black Bart; **Wild Bill Hickok:** Joseph G. Rosa; **Black-Faced Charley Bryant, Bat Masterson & Jim Courtright:** Robert K. DeArment; **Luke Short:** Wayne Short; **Ed Short:** Robert Ernst; **The Daltons:** Robert Barr Smith, Nancy B. Samuelson, John J. Kinney, Mark Boardman; **Pike Landusky and the Wild Bunch:** Gary A. Wilson; **Thompson Brothers:** Tom and Natalie Bicknell, Jim Gray; **Texas Saloons:** Richard Selcer; **Medicine Lodge:** Bill O'Neal, Rod Cook, Dillman Ash, Beverly McCollom, Len Gratteri; **Jesse Evans:** Chuck Parsons, Grady E. McCright, James H. Powell; **The Youngers:** Marley Brant, Wilbur Zink; **Apache Kid:** Phyllis Morreale-de la Garza, Dan L. Thrapp, Doug Hamilton; **John Selman:** Leon Metz; **Custer:** Jim Hatzell, Michael Donahue, Richard A. Fox, Jr., Kenneth Hammer, Col. W.A. Graham, Richard G. Hardorff; **Jeff Milton:** J. Evetts Haley, Don Chaput; **Zip Wyatt:** Glenn Shirley; **Bill Doolin:** Glenn Shirley; Col. Bailey C. Hanes; **Salt War:** Paul Cool.

Getting the Right Look: Models & Re-enactors

The following have modeled for my illustrations in this volume: **Outlaws & Lawmen:** Charles Motley, Todd Masden, Jackie Masden, Alexander Curtis, Jerry Guerich, Von Guerich, Jennie Smith, Flint Carney, DeAnne Giago and Steve "Handy" Rinsem; **Billy the Kid:** Mike Murphy, Jeff Smith, Tim Bell, William H. Cox, John T. Holbrook, Tony Tullis, Jeremiah Douglas and Thomas Bell; **Wild Bill Hickok:** Thadd Turner, Jerry Terantino, Jerry Crandall and Doc Ingalls; **Peppin Posse:** Thunderbolt, Richard Dobberstein, Gary Lehmann, Jim Fowler, Barb Kemp, David Dixon, Ruth Dixon and Big Ed Douglas; **Arizona Territorial Shooters:** Philip Carlin, Dan Jewell and Ross Seymour; **Pike Landusky Fight:** Bryan Bash, Rick Curry, Tammy Bash, Bryce Cornatzer, Darrell Goddard, Andrew Johnson, Sandy Curry, Don Bash, Darrell Keill, Mark Ball, Karin Lancaster, Tom Moore and Garrett Randolph (the kid kneeling in front, below). Also, thanks to Steve and Preston Randolph of Cactus Productions who put together the shoot in Cody, Wyoming, and to Neil LaFave of Studio 21 Photography for the great photo.

Thanks Everyone!

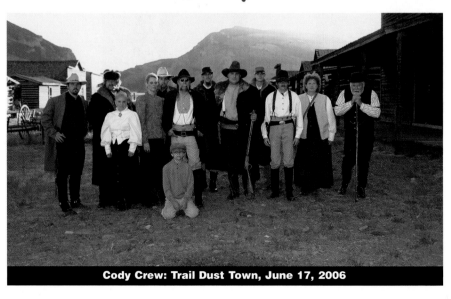

Cody Crew: Trail Dust Town, June 17, 2006